MY STORY

BY

Ron Kray

WITH

FRED DINENAGE

PAN BOOKS

First published 1993 by Sidgwick and Jackson

This edition published 1994 by Pan Books
an imprint of Pan Macmillan Ltd
Pan Macmillan, 20 New Wharf Road, London N1 9RR
Basingstoke and Oxford
Associated companies throughout the world
www.panmacmillan.com

ISBN 0 330 33507 3

Copyright © Fred Dinenage and Ron Kray 1993

The right of Fred Dinenage and Ron Kray to be identified as
the authors of this work has been asserted by them in
accordance with the Copyright, Designs and Patents Act 1988.

9

A CIP catalogue record for this book is available from
the British Library.

Typeset by Cambridge Composing (UK) Limited, Cambridge
Printed and bound in Great Britain by
Mackays of Chatham plc, Chatham, Kent

I dedicate my story to my wife Kate,
my brother Reg,
and my friends Irene Hart, John Griffiths, Mal Kirk,
Charlie Smith, Dot Welsh, Geraldine Charles,
Wilf Pine, and Stephanie King.

OUR MUM

Mum you are like a rose.
When God picked you, you were the best mum
   he could have chose.
You kept us warm when it was cold
With your arms around us you did fold.
For us you sold your rings of gold.
When you died, I like a baby cried.
When I think of you it is with pride,
So go to sleep mum I know that you are tired.

God pays debts without money.
Our dearest mother always used to say that.
I believe it. I have to.

Ron Kray

Contents

Fred Dinenage is a former journalist. He was the main presenter on two Olympic Games for ITV; for nine years he was main presenter on *Coast to Coast*, the TVS nightly news programme which twice won the Royal Television Society award for Best Regional News Programme. No other programme has ever won this award twice. He was also main presenter on *Meridian Tonight*, the nightly news programme in the south produced by Meridian Television. In February 1994 this too was named by the Royal Television Society as Best Regional Programme in Britain. He was co-author, with Reg and Ron Kray, of *Our Story*.

Prologue

They were the best years of our lives. They called them the Swinging Sixties. The Beatles and the Rolling Stones were the rulers of pop music, Carnaby Street ruled the fashion world . . . and me and my brother ruled London. We were fucking untouchable.

Nothing happened, especially in east London, that we didn't know about first. No crime was committed unless we said okay. If anyone in our 'manor' had a problem, they would come to us. They knew we would sort it. I'll give you an example. One day a friend of mine called 'Buller' Ward came to see me. He told me his son's nose had been broken in three places by a feller called Billy Blake. I knew about Blake. He was a flash, arrogant bastard; he was a bully. Not only had he disfigured the kid, but the lippy bastard was going around the East End boasting about hurting this kid.

The boy's father was upset about it. He didn't see how it was that Blake was getting away with it. He told the police but they didn't want to know. So I phoned this bully, Blake. I told

1

him I wanted to see him about some business. I told him to meet me in a club which we owned. I knew he would come, because he was greedy and he could smell money.

When he came into the club I grabbed him round the throat with my left hand, and with my right I pushed a white-hot poker down the side of his face. He screamed like a stuffed pig, and I could smell the flesh on his face burning.

At the time Blake and some people like him in the East End were starting to take liberties. So I made an example of him. He had to be shown that you never hurt women, or children, or old people. Or anyone who isn't involved in the underworld.

And you never crossed me or my brother, Reg.

Blake was lucky. I could have killed him. I have killed a man, and so has my brother. We've paid a high price for it – half our fucking lives, locked away. Was it worth it? I don't know. We just did what we had to do. It was all a long time ago.

But people still remember us, don't they?

Introduction

A judge called Melford Stevenson made his name when he
sent me and my brother down for thirty years. It made him
the most feared judge in Britain. He loved it.

But he lived to regret it. He paid for it with a gypsy's curse
that cost him his sight.

Melford Stevenson was an old bastard. It wasn't the terrible
sentence that upset us. We weren't surprised at that because our
lawyers had told us we'd get at least twenty years. No, what
upset us was the way he showed us no respect, no dignity. He
treated us worse than animals. During the trial he tried to make
us wear placards, pieces of card with our names on, hung round
our necks by a piece of string. Just like cattle at a market.

I wasn't having any of that. I told him to go and fuck
himself. Later, I got a Romany friend of mine to put a curse on
him. Not long after that he went blind. The Romany is a good
friend of mine. I'll call her Dot, I won't give her proper name.
But she said that Melford Stevenson was a spiteful and vindictive
man, and so she cursed him. He went blind, and later he died.

Melford Stevenson paid for not showing us respect, but he was never the all-powerful figure he thought he was. No. It took people far more powerful than him to bring our Firm down. It took the full might of the British government to do that. The government had to bring us down. They feared us, they couldn't control us, and they knew we were getting too powerful. We controlled London. We ran the gambling, the clubs, we knew about everyone and everything. We had MPs and lords and churchmen in our pockets, but we never took advantage of the likes of MPs like Tom Driberg, or lords like Effingham and Boothby. We could have done, though.

Harold Wilson and his government knew they had to smash us or, in the end, we would destroy them. It really was them or us. We were beginning to cause mayhem. They tried everything. They set the Fraud Squad on us, Scotland Yard, even the Inland Revenue. They thought the tax men would bring us down, just like they did Al Capone in America. But even that failed. It looked like we were indestructible.

In the end the police only brought us down because of the weakness of the men around us. And because of a pack of lies. In the end we were done because the police were more corrupt than we were.

Harold Wilson must have breathed a sigh of relief when we were put away. We scared him and his mates shitless. I remember going for a drink one night at Quaglino's, a club in the West End. I stood at the bar and noticed Harold Wilson was sat on the stool next to me, talking to another man. Wilson looked round and saw me. He put his drink down and fucked off out. He couldn't get out quick enough.

At that time me and my brother Reg could've bought Harold Wilson and his bloody cabinet ten times over. We had earned millions. Millions. And we gave most of it away, to charity and to people who needed it. Me and Reg never worried about money. If we wanted it we just went and got it.

CHAPTER ONE

The Early Years

I can remember precisely the moment my mental illness started, the moment I first became mad. I was twenty-two and in Wandsworth Prison, in London, doing three years on a charge of GBH (Grievous Bodily Harm). They said I'd beaten up a man called Terry Martin in a pub called the Britannia, in Stepney.

I was doing all right at Wandsworth. Then, one day, a prison warder came into my cell and told me, completely matter-of-factly, 'Kray, your auntie Rose is dead.' The news just shattered me. My auntie Rose was my mother's sister and we had always been very close, she had been good to me when I was a kid. But I never got any sympathy or understanding from that screw. I'll never forget what the bastard said when he saw how upset I was. He said, 'Well, she was getting on, wasn't she?' Getting on? My auntie was only in her forties. I could have killed him. But you do get some real bad bastards working in prisons.

When I heard about my auntie Rose it completely turned my mind. I got very depressed, I really went downhill. They sent me to Camp Hill, a soft prison on the Isle of Wight, but that made it worse because I felt far away from London and my family. I became withdrawn and very disorientated and had a breakdown. They sent me to the psychiatric wing of Winchester prison, but I couldn't get my mind straight, I couldn't get things under control. Once they even had to put me in a strait-jacket.

They certified me insane in February 1958, and sent me to Long Grove Mental Hospital, as it was then called, at Epsom in Surrey. I escaped from there and gradually began to sort myself out. But I know I've never been right in the head, not since that bastard told me my auntie Rose was dead. I've had problems ever since.

Once, when I was a kid, aged about ten, I thought about trying to commit suicide, but that was different. I'd had a row with my twin brother, Reg, and it had upset me. Even though we were identical twins and we were very close, we were different in many ways. Reg was always a mixer, always had a lot of mates around him. Me, I was more of a loner. I wasn't bothered so much about the other kids. I preferred to go off with my Alsatian, Freda, walking across the bomb sites in the East End of London, seeing what we could find. Anyway, one day me and Reg had had a row and I stood on top of a roof overlooking a tube train yard near our house in Vallance Road and I thought I would chuck myself down on to the railway lines and under the wheels of a train, but I never did it.

Really, we had a happy childhood. We were poor and it was hard, but it was the same for everyone in the East End in those days. We were born on Tuesday, 24 October 1933, in Stene Street, Hoxton, which is now called Shoreditch. Reggie was born at eight in the morning and I was born ten minutes later. We were identical twins except for a mole below the collar line on my neck. It was the only way you could tell us apart.

We had an older brother, Charlie, who was born in 1927. We should also have had a sister. Our parents did have a daughter, named Violet after our mother, but she died when she was a baby. It would have been nice to have had a sister, but thousands of kids died in the East End in those pre-war days. I read somewhere that out of every thousand kids born, more than a hundred never reached their fifth birthday. Pneumonia and tuberculosis were the biggest killers, and diphtheria and malnutrition caused a lot of deaths. Both me and Reg caught diphtheria when we were quite young. Reggie recovered okay but our mother was really worried about me and she brought me home from hospital and nursed me herself.

Before the war we moved from Hoxton, one mile south across the Hackney Road, to 178 Vallance Road, in Bethnal Green. Number 178 isn't there any more, they knocked it down for new development, but it was a little bit bigger and better than our other house. It was just part of a terrace but we always thought it was a lucky house.

I can remember it had a big coal fire in the kitchen which we used to sit in front of while our mother did the ironing. I can remember the big viaducts, covered in soot, which stood above all the houses. I can remember the trains which used to go along the lines at the end of our backyard on their way in and out of Liverpool Street station. And I can remember lying in bed early in the mornings in the back bedroom me and Reg used to share, listening to our mum singing in the backyard as she hung out the washing. She had a lovely voice. Our mother was always happy, even though she had to struggle so hard and times were really bad for us and the other families in the East End.

Our father was called Charles, though everyone knew him as Charlie. He made his living as what they called a 'pesterer'. He would go around the better areas buying bits of gold and silver, and sometimes clothing, which he would then re-sell for a profit. He was very good at it.

Our parents weren't what you'd call religious, but they did encourage me and Reg to pray. We would pray for the sick and the suffering and the weak people all over the world, and for our family and friends. Over the years, in my time spent in prisons and institutions, I've come up against a lot of flash, big-headed so-called hard cases who have scorned and ridiculed people who believe in prayer. I've always put this down to their own ignorance because some of the greatest people in the history of the world have believed in the power of prayer. People like Winston Churchill, Lawrence of Arabia, Gordon of Khartoum, Admiral Nelson and John Brown, who helped free the slaves. And great men I have known personally have believed in the power of God, including two heavyweight boxing champions of the world, Joe Louis and Muhammad Ali. And many leading men in the Mafia have also been great believers. I know this because they have told me.

Our parents also encouraged us to be kind to animals. We kept chickens in the backyard and, just after we started school, we had a little mongrel dog which used to come and meet us from school.

About the same time me and Reg went to the cinema to see a film called *Lassie the Sheepdog*. We liked it so much that when we came home we put olive oil on our mongrel's coat and brushed him till he shone, and we changed his name to Lassie. I have always loved all animals and I get furious at the stories I've heard saying that I am cruel to them. I would not like anyone to believe I would ever hurt or mistreat an animal.

When me and Reg were young we used to like to listen to the radio and our favourite programmes were *Dick Barton, Special Agent*, *Just William* and *Forces Favourites*. With our mother, we would also sit and listen to *Mrs Dale's Diary*, which was about a doctor's family.

The first school we went to was Wood Close School, in Brick Lane, which was near to our home in Vallance Road. There was a pub on the corner of Brick Lane, which we used to pass every day on our way to school. It was called the Carpenter's Arms and, many years later, we bought this pub. We were happy at school, and also at Daniel Street School, where we went to later.

We weren't brilliant but we weren't dunces, either. We were

both good at sport, and good at fighting. There were quite a few scraps and the kids in our street used to have brick battles against gangs of kids from other streets. It was a tough area and they used to say that if you came from the East End you finished up either a villain, a thief, or a fighter. Most people finished up one of those three things. Me and Reg had a pact – we decided we were going to be fighters, to try and make our names in the boxing ring. But if it didn't work out, we had made up our minds to be villains.

There were some good fighters in our family. Our grandfather on our mother's side was called John Lee. He was also known as the Southpaw Cannonball, because he could punch so hard, especially with his left hand. He lived over a café he owned on the other side of Vallance Road. Even when he was an old man he used to enjoy punching an old mattress slung over a clothes line in the backyard. When we were small, he used to put me and Reg on his knee and tell us stories about the East End and its great fighting men. Our heroes were always fighters. The greatest of them all was Ted 'Kid' Lewis, who was champion of the world at three different weights. He grew up near our home in Vallance Road, but even though he was a big name he never forgot his roots and his old friends. We also admired the famous local villains, men like Jimmy Spinks, Timmy Hayes, Dodger Mullins and Wassle Newman. They were like legends in the East End.

Our family life was based around Vallance Road. Our mother's two sisters lived in the two houses next to ours. They were Auntie Rose and Auntie May. I was very fond of them both, especially my auntie Rose. She was as tough as any man, tougher than most, but with me she was always very gentle. My auntie Rose knew about things. One day at school some kids had been taking the mickey out of me because my eyebrows seemed different to theirs. Mine seemed to go straight across the bridge of my nose, without a gap in the middle. I came home from school and told my auntie Rose what had happened. I asked her why my eyebrows were like that. She said to me, 'It means you were born to hang, Ronnie love.'

That was one thing the film about us, *The Krays*, got right. But they got a lot of things wrong, they made them up. I have not been allowed to see the film in Broadmoor but other people have told me exactly what was in it. The film was released in 1990 and it was very successful. It was a big hit, they tell me, in America. But, like I say, they got many things wrong. There is a scene with me and Reg talking to my auntie Rose about a dream we have had, about a bird with no wings which flies up into the sun. This never happened. In another scene a teacher asks me to give him a 'wonderful word', and I say to him, 'Crocodile.' This, also, never happened. Neither did we ever shoot up a pub with machine guns. These things did not happen but, because it is in a film, some people believe it.

What they never touched on in the film was the event which changed all our lives – the Second World War. For a start, our father wasn't around. He was called up, and ordered to report to the Tower of London. But our father wasn't having any of that, so he went on the trot, and he was on the run from the army for the next twelve years. It's a funny thing, but when he and all the absconders got their amnesty from the Queen, me and Reg were on the run from the army ourselves.

With our father away life was very hard for our mother. A lot of the time he was away he spent at the house of a friend of his in south London, a pickpocket called Bob Rolphe. We would go and see him sometimes, with our mother, and take him clean clothes and food. Sometimes he would come home for a day or two, and before he left he would send me and Reg down to the corner shop to make sure there were no police around. Once when he was at Vallance Road the police came. He was hiding in the coal cellar and one of the policemen was going to open the door leading down to it. I said to him, 'Our dad is not a fool, he wouldn't hide down there, would he?' And the policeman shrugged his shoulders and turned away. But the police made us hate them in those times. They were always coming round to our house, banging on the door in the early hours of the morning, waking everybody up, looking for our father. But they never found him. I hated the police and I hated Hitler and the Germans. They destroyed ten thousand houses in Bethnal Green alone, and they killed and injured hundreds of innocent people.

Once a bomb fell underneath the railway arch half-way down Vallance Road and, as it exploded, it demolished a block of flats. Our own house shook and things went flying. Me and Reg were thrown out of our beds. A lot of people were killed and some were trapped underneath the rubble. I can remember the firemen and the rescuers tearing at the bricks and mortar with their bare hands, trying to get people out.

The war was exciting for me. I can remember the glare of the big searchlights looking for German bombers, for dogfights in the sky, the explosions, the fires. Our mother used to tell us to pray for the war to end. I was praying for Hitler to get smashed by a bus, but our mother told me it was wrong to pray for things like that, even though Hitler was a bad man. When the air-raid siren went off our mother would grab me and Reg and our brother Charlie and take us to the air-raid shelter under the viaduct. It was nice in there, with fires going, and everyone was friendly. Our grandfather, John Lee, used to put on a show on a little wooden stage. He would lick a white-hot poker and balance on a pile of bottles which he placed on top of one another to form a sort of glass wall. There was dancing and music and singing and every time a train passed over the top of the viaduct the whole place would shake and fill with black smoke.

For a time we were evacuated to a farm out in the country, at Hadleigh in Suffolk. We loved it, me and Reg, running in the fields, breathing in the air and seeing the animals. Our mother didn't like it so much, away from the East End, but me and Reg, we liked the country.

When we are free again we both want to live in the country. In the sixties we bought a nice house at Bildeston, which is a village only about four miles from Hadleigh. We gave the house to our mother but she had to sell it when we were put away and the money started to run out. It was a pity because it is worth a lot of money today. Funny enough, someone sent my wife an estate agent's particulars, recently, advertising a house they were selling at Bildeston. There was a photograph of the house on the front. Yes, it was The Brooks, the house that me and Reg used to own. This is how they described it:

A SUBSTANTIAL VICTORIAN COUNTRY HOUSE
ENJOYING A SECLUDED VILLAGE SETTING.
FIVE BEDS, TWO BATHS, FULL CENTRAL HEATING
AND DOUBLE-GLAZING; AN ANNEXE COTTAGE,
STABLING AND STORAGE ROOM;
POOL, GARDENS, PADDOCK.
OFFERS INVITED IN THE REGION OF
£295,000 FREEHOLD.

Looking at the photograph brought back some nice memories. It would have been a good place for me and Reg to retire to. We both love Suffolk.

When we went back to London we used to make some money by selling firewood. Some days we would get up very early and go out with our uncle, Joe Lee, our mother's brother, to Billingsgate fish market where he worked. He used to turn up outside our house at four in the morning with his cart pulled by Shire horses.

Some days we would go on a pony and trap with a man called Harry Hopwood, who used to buy and sell rags and woollens. Harry Hopwood was a friend of our father. He used to sit us on his knee and try and get us to drink from a bottle of brown ale. He seemed a good man, but he turned against us later. Years later he was a prosecution witness against us. He died an alcoholic. Maybe he turned to the drink because he had bad things on his conscience.

When we were twelve, the war ended. We started back at school, at Daniel Street. To earn a bit of money we used to help our grandfather, Jimmy Kray, on his old clothes stall in Brick Lane. We used to keep an eye on his cash box while he was selling the clothes. And when we were twelve we had our first trouble with the law. Or Reg did, anyway. We had been with some friends to Chingford, in Essex, for a picnic. On the way back, on the train, Reg fired a few shots from his slug gun out of the window. A slug gun is similar to an air pistol. He wasn't trying to hit anybody, but the guard stopped the train and locked Reg in his cabin. When we got back to London the Transport Police were waiting. They made something out of nothing and even took Reg to court. They treated him like a hardened criminal. He got off with a warning after the Reverend Hetherington spoke up for him.

The Reverend R. H. Hetherington was a man we had respect for. He ran a youth club in the Bethnal Green Road, which we joined. He was a tall and powerful man and he knew how to deal with East End kids. He even had us running errands for him. Sometimes we went to his church and I remember he had such a clear and powerful voice. He was a good friend to us over many years and he spoke as a character witness for us more than once. He also presided at our mother's funeral.

The boxing started when we were about twelve, too. Our mother let us have a room at Vallance Road, which we turned into a small gym, and our older brother Charlie started to teach us some boxing technique. Charlie was in the navy by now and he was quite a good boxer. He let us have a navy kitbag which we stuffed full of rags and old clothes and used as a punch ball. It was suspended from the ceiling by a hook, and held down by a meat hook in the floor boards. One night our father crept into the room after he'd had a few drinks and the meat hook went straight through his foot. He was in agony, but we all had a good laugh.

A lot of the local kids used our homemade gym, including a

kid called Kenny Lynch, who later made his name as a singer, and the Gill brothers, the Nicholson brothers and Charlie Page, who all became pro fighters. Most people know the story of how me and Reg sort of made our professional début. A travelling fair came to Bethnal Green, in Turin Street. The big attraction for us was the Alf Stewart boxing booth where one pound was offered to any man who could go three rounds with one of the fighters on the booth. It wasn't easy because the fighters they had, Buster and Steve Osbourne, Les Haycox and Slasher Warner, could handle themselves. On the opening night there weren't many takers, so Alf Stewart said he would pay any spectators who would get in the ring and fight each other. Me and Reg shouted out that we would fight. And we did. We had a good scrap for three rounds. Reg's face was bruised and my nose was bleeding. But the crowd enjoyed it and Alf Stewart gave us seven shillings and sixpence (about thirty-five pence in today's currency), which was a lot of money then. That was something else the film got wrong. In the film, they tell me, our grandfather, John Lee, is seen in the ring in the boxing booth. And he's getting a pasting, which is why me and Reg wanted to fight. That never happened, our grandfather didn't fight at the boxing booth.

But another fighter, Charlie Simms, saw us and he thought we had some talent. He persuaded us to join the Robert Browning boxing club and he became our trainer. By the time we were fifteen, in 1948, Reggie won the London Schoolboys' Championship, was a Great Britain Schoolboys' Championship finalist, South East Divisional Youth Club Champion and London ATC Champion. I won the Hackney Schoolboys' Championship, a London Junior Championship and a London ATC title. We even got in the newspapers. One paper said, 'The Kray twins could go on to become as famous as another pair of sporting twins, the cricketers Alec and Eric Bedser.'

It was at this time, when we were fifteen, that I was in a film. I was in the famous Repton boxing club, one night, when another man who was there, a film director, said he needed extras for a film he was making at Ealing Studios. The film was called *The Magic Box*, starring Robert Donat, and me and a friend called Shaun Venables were in it. So was the great boxer Jack 'Kid' Berg but I never spoke to him then. Many years later he became a friend of ours and used to come to our clubs. We were very sad when he died in 1991. *The Magic Box* was shown by BBC Television in 1991 and a friend of mine saw it and recognized me – even though I was only on the screen for a few seconds! My friend took a photo of me in the film as he watched it on his TV set. I was pleased he still recognized me after all these years!

By the time we were sixteen me and Reg had our own gang. Most kids in the area belonged to gangs because it was such a tough area. We also carried weapons when we went to dances and so on, because if other gangs knew you were tooled up you were less likely to get bother. I was given a gun at about this time, but I never used it. We used to keep our weapons hidden under the floorboards at Vallance Road and if we got wind that the police were coming to the house we would move them to friends' houses.

We got into a bit of bother after a fight outside a dance hall in Mare Street, in Hackney. We were charged with GBH against three men, Dennis Seigenberg, Walter Birch and Roy Harvey. Years later, in Parkhurst prison, Reg met up with Seigenberg again. By then he'd changed his name to Dennis Stafford and he'd been convicted of murder. We were sent to the number one court at the Old Bailey, in front of Judge McClure. The Reverend Hetherington spoke for us and we were acquitted through lack of evidence. At the end of the trial the judge said to us, 'Don't go around thinking you are the Sabini brothers.' The Sabinis were well-known gangsters at the time and later they became friends when one of the brothers, Johnny Sabini, used to visit me in Broadmoor. Our good relationship with the Reverend Hetherington carried on through the years. He was a fine man and he gave us a lot of good advice. I remember he once told me that he

ver once saw an instance of a person who was dying who failed
to turn to God. I had proof of this with my own uncle Albert, my
auntie May's husband, who was one of the kindest, gentlest men
I ever met. He, too, turned to God, and his last words to my
auntie, before he died, were, 'I am not a wicked man, am I,
May?'

Father Hetherington used to say to me, 'You don't have to
go to church, but you must believe in the Creator. You must find
time to think about Him.' I think that is why many people in
prisons and hospitals like Broadmoor turn to God. They have
the time to think, to analyse their lives. I know, because it has
happened to me.

We had no more trouble with the police for another year.
Nineteen fifty, when we were seventeen, we were still doing our
boxing, and doing well, and we did some work, mainly in the
markets. Shifting boxes around gave us a bit of money and
helped to build our muscles. When the next trouble with the
police came it wasn't really our fault. I was standing with Reg
and some friends outside a café in the Bethnal Green Road. A
policeman told us to move along. Then he gave me a shove in
the back. I hit him. We ran off, but the police came looking for
us. When they tried to arrest me, Reg became involved as well.
We both got charged with assault. We were lucky. The Reverend
Hetherington spoke up for us again, and we got probation.

A few months later, we both turned professional as boxers.
We weighed an identical nine stones, nine pounds – we were
lightweights – and we both did well. We won our first fights at
the Mile End Arena. Reg beat Bob Manito, from Clapham, and
I knocked out Bernie Long, from Romford. In all, Reg had
seven fights as a pro and he won them all. I had six fights, won
four and lost two. Our older brother Charlie turned pro, too,
and he did well, winning twenty-one out of twenty-five fights.
They used to call him Evergreen Charlie Kray and he was a
stylish fighter. I've only ever seen him lose his temper once, and
that was when he knocked out a fellow called Jimmy Cornell, in

the first club we owned called the Double R. Jimmy Cornell had a brother called George. I had to kill him later.

I think we could have gone all the way as boxers, but then they called us up for the army. We were ordered to report to the Tower of London to join the Royal Fusiliers. We didn't want to go in the army, but we hoped they would let us be PTIs (Physical Training Instructors). They didn't, of course. The next two years were a waste of time. We spent them either escaping, or locked up in the guardhouse. Once, when we were in the guardroom at the Tower, our father came to see us. He was still on the trot himself, so he had to come in disguise. Nobody recognized him. I have some happy memories of my father. He was a good man when he wasn't in drink. Once, when I was a boy, he was going off to the bookmaker's, and he said to me, 'Go on, Ron, choose a horse and I'll put a quid on it.' I looked at the runners in his newspaper and I picked a horse called Gay Donald. It won at thirty-three to one. So I'd won thirty-three pounds, which was a lot of money in them days.

Once, when we were on the run, we borrowed a car and drove to Southend for the weekend with a friend of ours. We sent the commanding officer at the Tower a postcard saying, 'Wish you were here. Reg and Ron Kray.' He had a sense of humour and he pinned the card to his office wall. Another time when we were on the run the police arrested us and put us on an identification parade. They said they suspected us of attacking a man with a truncheon and stabbing him with a knife. We were not picked out on the parade so the police handed us back to the army.

Another time we were in a café in the Mile End Road when a policeman began to get aggressive. So I hit him and Reg got involved as well. We were sent before Thames Magistrates. They gave us a month's jail for assaulting a policeman and we were sent to Wormwood Scrubs. At the end of that month, on Good Friday 1953 when we were nineteen, they decided to send us to the army barracks at Canterbury, in Kent, to be court-martialled. We went down there by train, handcuffed to military policemen.

...en we got to Canterbury Barracks we overpowered the guards and escaped. It was easy.

We were arrested twenty-four hours later at Eltham, in the suburbs of south London. They took us back to Canterbury where we were later court-martialled and sent to the glasshouse at Shepton Mallet in the West Country. That's the place where they shot some of the film, *The Dirty Dozen*. It was very hard there. Among the people we met was Charlie Richardson, who later ran his own gang with his brother in south London. We gave as good as we got at Shepton Mallet. Once we smashed the guardhouse up; then we set fire to it.

Finally, when we were twenty, they let us out of the army. We had no money and no jobs. Because of our records we had no real chance, now, of making it in boxing. But we still had the pact we had made when we were young: if we couldn't make it as fighters, then we'd make it as villains.

CHAPTER TWO

The Living Years . . .

The first thing me and Reg did when they slung us out of the army was to go and see a friend of ours called Billy Jones. They called Billy 'The Fox', and he and a feller called Bobby Ramsey ran a club called Stragglers in Cambridge Circus in the West End. Billy said he'd give us a few quid to tide us over and we'd do odd jobs in return, a bit of bouncing, that sort of thing. It was fine for a while, just while we sorted ourselves out, and we were grateful to Billy. He stayed a good friend of ours and we were sorry when he died recently.

But me and Reg wanted to better ourselves. We were only a couple of working-class lads from the East End, we'd both been in bits of bother with the law and we'd both been booted out of the army. I suppose you could call us undesirables! You could say we were going nowhere fast. But still we fancied ourselves. We were young, we were fit, and if we weren't exactly well educated we were very street-wise.

The turning point for us came when we heard about a billiard hall in the Mile End Road. It was known as a real ouble-spot: there were a lot of fights there and the place was always getting smashed up. We heard the lease was up for grabs, so we went and saw the man who owned it, Mr Martin. He said to us, 'No one has been able to handle this place. What makes you two think you can do different?'

I said to him, 'If you let us have this place, if any fighting starts, we'll stop it. There'll be no more trouble, and you'll get your money every week.' So he said, right, he'd try it. We were as good as our word. We smashed a few heads together and the fighting stopped – and Mr Martin got his rent. We called it the Regal and turned it into a really nice place, with fourteen tables and a bar.

John Pearson, who wrote the first book about us, said the Regal was a run-down snooker hall with two tables. It wasn't. That was one of a lot of things about us he and other people got wrong. People have said that me and Reg were behind most of the trouble at the Regal, that we started a lot of the bother ourselves, just so that we could get our hands on the lease. They even said that the feller who had the lease before us used to keep an Alsatian behind the bar to frighten off trouble-makers, and that we used to chuck fireworks over the bar to drive the dog mad.

None of it is true. We got the lease because Mr Martin could see that we were just about the only fellers who could deal with all the trouble at his club. It was as simple as that. It wasn't easy, and it was at the Regal that we came face to face with the protection racket for the first time. Protection was rife in London at the time and I expect it still is in towns and cities everywhere. The Chinese communities do it a lot. All it is, a gang will threaten to damage a property or a business unless the owner agrees to pay them money not to. Then, once the owner is paying money to the gang, the gang will make sure no other villains try to put any financial pressures on him. If they do, they will be sorted out. The club or business will be protected. Most people pay up to avoid trouble.

I was serving drinks behind the bar one afternoon when a Maltese gang walked in. One of them came up to the bar, asked me if I was running the club, and said he wanted to talk about business. I asked him what he wanted. He said in future he'd be coming in every week to collect protection money. If we didn't pay it, he said, the club could have a bit of trouble. What sort of trouble? Oh, you know, a few smashed windows, maybe a petrol bomb, a fire, a few of the cloths on the tables ripped, a big fight. That sort of thing.

I picked up a bayonet we kept behind the bar. I threw him across one of the billiard tables, and I stuck that bayonet straight through his hand. Pinned him to the table. It was him that needed protection then. There was now a right skirmish going on in the club, so I grabbed a Japanese sword we kept hung on the wall, took it down, and chased the rest of the Maltese bastards out of the club. They all jumped into a Ford car, but they couldn't get it started. So I started to smash it up with the sword. I smashed up the roof and the bonnet and the windscreen. In the end they were lucky: they managed to get the motor started and drive away. They were lucky because if they hadn't, I would have smashed them up as well. After that we never had no more trouble with protection gangs. But, like I always say, in our business you have to meet fire with fire. We were like soldiers, soldiers of the streets, defending our territory against the enemy. And that's all we ever did when it came to violence, we only ever fought with our own kind. So, we worked hard and we did well with the Regal.

It was about this time we started to go to a restaurant called the Vienna Rooms, just off the Edgware Road. A lot of well-known villains used to go there. It was a real meeting place for the top men. It was there we met two of the biggest men in the underworld, Jack Spot and Billy Hill. Both of them were powerful men. Jack Spot's real name was Jack Comer, but he was called Spot because he was always on the spot whenever a big crime was committed. He was from Aldgate. Billy Hill was from Camden Town, and he was The Man as far as me and Reg were concerned – tough, smart, violent if necessary, but with a great brain. He was a true professional. Both he and Spot were smart dressers and that also impressed me.

Jack Spot hired us to do a bit of work for him, keeping an eye on his bookmakers' pitches at racecourses, just in case other gangs tried to move in on them, or in case anyone tried to pinch the money. There wasn't a lot of trouble as it turned out, though me and Reg always had plenty of weapons in our car, just in case. We enjoyed the days at the races but we packed it in in the end because we had too many other things starting to go for us. The Regal was still doing well, but we had one or two other projects on the side. We could supply dockers' tickets, documents which would enable a man to work as a docker, earning big money for just a few hours' work. We used to sell these tickets for varying amounts, depending on what we thought a man could afford to pay. We had a nice little thing going with a doctor in the East End who would sign documents which got young lads out of doing National Service, which everyone hated. Lads and their parents used to pay us well for this service. And we were also involved in a little business bringing watches through London docks, unofficially. At that stage we were just two sharp fellers trying to get a bit of cash together so that we could buy one or two clubs and be legitimate. See, I think me and Reg would have been good businessmen. We both had brains in our heads and we were both hard workers. We probably wouldn't have been completely 'straight', but I don't think we were *destined* to be criminals. It wasn't really in the family, or anything like that. It just sort of happened.

We still liked a scrap, of course we did, and we sometimes used to get into little battles. We did it for fun, really. Reggie once worked out he'd broken eleven men's jaws in fights. See, me and Reg have always admired fighters, in the ring and out. We like men who are game. When we were younger we used to admire men like Billy Bligh and Tommy Smithson. Billy was from Clerkenwell, only a little feller, but he was as game as anything. He died in Wandsworth from a burst ulcer. Tommy Smithson was a well-known villain, a hard man who was shot to death by a Maltese gang. I would say he was game. I would say that the gamest men I've known would be Freddie Foreman, who did time with us, Jimmy Nash, and Frankie Fraser, who used to be with the Richardson gang. These are the sort of men we've always admired.

Me and Reg didn't really have any bother with the police till we were twenty-three. That was in 1957. Two friends of ours, who ran a club, had been having trouble with an Irish gang, and they weren't sure how to deal with it. The ringleader, I was told, was a feller called Terry Martin, so I thought I would go and sort him out. I was told that Terry Martin was drinking in a pub called the Britannia, in Stepney. I went round there and I found Martin playing cards with some other men in the saloon bar. I asked him to come outside, and we had a fight in the street. I hurt him, quite badly, because I thought he deserved it.

Martin was taken to hospital and the matter should have ended there. But, instead, when he was interviewed by the police in his hospital bed, Martin did the unforgivable thing – he broke the East End code of conduct and he grassed on me. The police, obviously, were out to get me, because they gave Martin protection and he later gave evidence against me at the Old Bailey. Mind you, he had to get out of London quickly as soon as the trial was over, and he never came back. He would have been in real trouble if he had.

I got sent down for three years on a charge of GBH. I remember the judge, Sir Gerald Dodson, who was the Recorder of London, saying to me in court: 'It would seem there has existed, for some time, a state of gang warfare, dangerous to all concerned.' It wasn't really gang warfare at all. Or, if it was, it was nothing like what it was going to be, when me and Reg really got going. But for the time being I was out of the game, and I was well pissed off about it. They sent me to Wandsworth and I was doing all right there, I was coping okay, until that bastard warder told me that my auntie Rose had died. I went into a state of real depression. I couldn't seem to get out of it. Wandsworth is a depressing place, anyway, but I was really bad. So they sent me to Camp Hill, a soft prison on the Isle of Wight, because, I suppose, they thought I might be happier there.

But I wasn't. It just felt a long way from London and Reg and the family. I got very withdrawn and disorientated, and I had a mental breakdown. I didn't know how ill I was, nor did they. They didn't know how to deal with it. They transferred me to the psychiatric wing at Winchester prison, but I just went out of control. I just wanted to smash everything and everybody. I couldn't seem to get me mind sorted. They certified me insane in February 1958. It was a bad time, a frightening experience. Once they even put me in a strait-jacket. No one could control me, I couldn't even control myself. They gave me drugs, but they seemed to make it worse. They didn't know what to do with me at Winchester, so they moved me to Long Grove Mental Hospital. When I was there I started to feel a bit better but I was surrounded by other people who were really ill in their heads, really sick. I felt sorry for them but I knew that I would not get better in a place like that. I knew I had to get out. Some people have said that I deliberately faked my mental illness just so I would get sent to Long Grove. It wasn't true. But I knew the doctors at Long Grove might not set me free for a long time. They could have kept me there as long as they liked, I could have stayed there a lot longer than the three years I was sent down for. Reg looked into it for me and he found out that if I managed to get out and stay out for more than fourteen days, then the doctors would have to re-examine me to see if I was fit enough to be released at the proper time. That was the law. So we worked out a good scam to get me out.

Reg and three other friends came to visit me. They were brought into the locked ward which I shared with several other patients. Reg was wearing a similar navy blue suit to the one I was wearing, and a similar grey check shirt, blue tie and black shoes. At the end of visiting time it was me who walked out of the hospital with our three friends, and Reggie who was sat in the ward reading a newspaper. Of course, they didn't realize that until I was well clear and Reggie demanded to be let out. There was a bit of argy-bargy with the police, who had no choice but to let him go with a few threats about prosecuting him. Like I said, I only needed to be out for fourteen days, but I liked it better outside so I stayed out for a hundred and forty-five days. I lived most of the time in Suffolk, in a caravan on a farm owned by a friend of ours, but sometimes I came back to London. A few times I even slept in my own bed in Vallance Road. The police eventually found me there, took me back to Long Grove, where the doctors re-examined me and said I was a lot better. I stayed there for a bit more observation, then they moved me back to Wandsworth, and eventually released me in the spring of 1959. They said I should have some more treatment as an out-patient at a mental hospital in London, but I only went a few times because I didn't think it was doing me any good. I was feeling a lot better. I still had bad times, but not so many.

While I'd been away, Reg had been busy. He had found some premises in the Bow Road which he turned into our club the Double R. It was a drinking and gambling club, and it was very successful. On the night it opened he sent me a telegram at Wandsworth. With some help from our brother Charlie he'd also bought a couple of spiels, illegal drinking clubs. Small, not very attractive places, but they made good money from people who wanted to drink out of hours. Over the years we owned about thirty-four different clubs and spiels, but I think I liked the Double R best of all. I liked it partly because it was our first club and partly because downstairs it had a fully equipped gym where we used to meet a lot of our friends from the boxing world. Henry Cooper, one of the greatest heavyweights this country has ever produced, did the opening ceremony for us. We knew all the big names of boxing, including Billy Walker, another famous heavyweight fighter.

Me and Reg also really liked the Kentucky club, in the Mile End Road in Stepney, which we opened in 1963. It was a really plush place with lots of red velvet and big mirrors. In the swinging sixties the Kentucky was one of the 'in' places to be.

By the early sixties me and Reg had collected a gang. We didn't set out to do it, it just happened. Fellers used to hang around with us and they just sort of stayed. We became known as the Firm. I never really liked us being called that, I always thought it was a name that could backfire on us one day. Why? Well, the Firm implies that something is well organized, and the police never like to think criminals are well organized. It's better to try and keep a low profile. During our trial at the Old Bailey in 1969, the prosecution lawyers kept using the word, and one of them asked me: 'Is it right that you and your gang are known as the Firm?' I took out a small dictionary I always kept in my pocket, found the right page, and said to him: 'The word Firm means commercial enterprise. Well, I'm out of work and I haven't got a factory or any other commercial enterprise, so it looks like you're wrong.' But we had put together a strong gang of men. Me and Reg were the leaders and under us we had men like Ian Barrie, Pat Connolly, Tommy 'The Bear' Brown, Big Albert Donaghue, Sammy Lederman, Cornelius 'Connie' White-head, Ronnie Bender, Tony and Chrissie Lambrianou, Scotch Jack Dickson, Ronnie Hart, and many more. Some did a lot of work for us, some did little. Some were important, some weren't. Nearly all of them, with the exception of Ian Barrie, let us down in the end, grassed on us and told lies about us, just to save their own skins.

Apart from the clubs, we had plenty of other things going. One of the best earners was a little scam called the Long-term Fraud. How it worked was so simple. We'd rent a warehouse in a phoney name and set up a phoney company in the names of

other people. We'd begin to order stuff from major suppliers –
televisions, washing machines, furniture, that sort of thing. We'd
only order small amounts, and make sure they were paid
promptly. This would go on for some months until we'd got the
confidence of the suppliers, then we'd order enough stuff to fill
the warehouse. Then, wallop, we'd sell off the lot quickly and
fairly cheaply – and disappear. It never failed. Instant cash, and
no trouble.

Mind you, if there ever was any trouble, we were well
equipped to deal with it. We had gradually got together a real
arsenal of weapons which we kept in various safe places. The
thing that made us different from most gangs in London in those
days was that we weren't afraid to use them. I've shot several
people over the years. The first person I shot was an ex-boxer
called Shorty, who was trying to put the squeeze for protection
money on a friend of ours who owned a garage. Shorty didn't
know this feller was a friend of ours, of course. When Shorty
went to the garage to collect his money, he found me there
waiting for him. He started to get lippy, made a couple of threats,
so I shot him in the leg with an automatic Luger. The police
arrested me and put me on an identification parade, but Shorty
wasn't stupid and he didn't pick me out.

Another time, a feller called George Dixon upset me in a
club, and I tried to kill him. I took out my Luger, aimed it at his
head and pulled the trigger. Dixon was lucky because the gun
jammed. He ran out of the club fucking quickly. It must have
been a million to one against the gun jamming. Later I made
friends with Dixon and gave him the bullet. I thought it would
be a good reminder to him to be careful about who he upset.
Another time, I was having a drink at the Central club, in
Clerkenwell, with an Italian feller by the name of Battles. This
club was a meeting place for all the Italians in London at the
time. While I was there I got into an argument with a feller by
the name of Billy Alco. I took my gun out of my pocket and took
a shot at Alco. Luckily I missed him and I'm pleased now I did

because he has become a good friend over the years and has come to see me at Broadmoor. People used to ask me why I was so unpredictable, so volatile. I didn't know then, but I think now it was my mental illness, my paranoia. I just couldn't stop myself from hurting people, especially if I thought they were slighting me or plotting against me. Also, I liked the feeling of guns.

Usually, though, I was happier with my fists or a knife. I had a lot of scraps with people, and I cut quite a few people with my knife. But we didn't set out to make people frightened of us, we like to think we got things out of people because they respected us, not because they feared us. I mean, another thing they always say about the Krays is that we ran all the big protection rackets in London. That's not true, we were never involved in protection, not as such. People are always saying we used to send our men round to clubs and restaurants and shops and threaten to smash them up unless they gave us money. But we never did that, we didn't have to. People used to come to us and ask us to look after their places, to keep other gangs away or small-time villains operating on their own. But we were never involved in protection. We never used to go to them and say, 'If you don't give us this money we'll smash your place up.' I deny that strongly. We had a reputation in the East End and the West End for looking after places. There were some who said we collected protection money but that is wrong, it's all lies. If people want to call it protection, they can, but it wasn't protection as we see it. If the people we helped wanted to give us gifts, that was up to them. Usually it was cigarettes or cases of drink but we never forced them. We didn't have to. We had so much money coming in, we were worth millions. Millions. We gave it all away. Money, jewellery, watches, rings, cuff-links, nights out on the town, cars, everything. We gave a lot of money to charity, and to boys' clubs, and of course we blew a lot of it on ourselves. Even the police were always trying to pin protection on us.

Shortly after I got out in 1959, the police stitched Reggie up on a money with menaces charge. A Polish feller called Murray

Podlo, who ran a shop in the Finchley Road, said Reg had threatened to cut him unless he gave him a hundred pounds. A hundred quid? For fuck's sake, at that time we were paying the doormen on our clubs more than that, we were giving away more than that in tips. Why would Reg have risked his freedom for such a small amount of money? It was a frame-up and Reg got eighteen months. Even though Podlo later retracted his evidence, Reg was still convicted and sent to Wandsworth.

But really the early sixties were a good time for us. Business was booming. We opened up more clubs, like the Green Dragon and Dodgers, in Whitechapel, we had several spiels doing good business, and we had pubs, including the Carpenters Arms, near Mile End underground station. We did that place up nicely with red-striped Regency wallpaper and plush red velvet seats. That was one of our favourite places. Me and Reg would go there often at nights, get out our contact books and ring around all our friends. They would come round and we would have some great boozy nights that finally ended up in the West End in the early hours of the next day. Me and Reg were big drinkers, we could drink spirits till the cows came home, but we could take it well, we didn't get really drunk very often. We turned the Carpenters into a sort of private club for us and our friends. Not everything we touched worked out, though. We lost a packet investing in a development project in a place called Enugu, in Nigeria, after Ernest Shinwell, the son of the Labour MP Manny Shinwell, had talked us into joining a consortium he had formed. It looked like a good thing at the time but it taught us a lesson: never get involved in things you can't control personally. It was like a seaside development, the sort of thing you get in Spain and places like that. You know, apartments, shops, offices, that sort of thing, for the wealthy Africans and, maybe, Europeans to go to. We put a lot of money into the thing, up front, because it seemed okay. But the money disappeared and we never got it back, and the project just disappeared. You know, it is difficult doing business with people like that. I went over to Nigeria to have a look. It wasn't much of a place but the people were very friendly. The feller showing me round asked me if there was anything I specially wanted to see. I said I would like to see their jail. It was terrible, it made Parkhurst look like a holiday camp. I couldn't wait to get out of the place.

We lost money with Shinwell, we also lost money when we got involved with Lord Effingham, though in both cases it wasn't their fault. We used Lord Effingham, alias Mowbray, Henry Gordon, Sixth Earl of Effingham, Lord Howard of Effingham, as our sort of front man in our first move into the West End. It was a gambling club called Esmerelda's Barn, a very upmarket place in Wilton Place, in Knightsbridge. We used a lot of our own money in that venture, none of it was Effie's, as we used to call him. He didn't have a lot of cash – in fact we were better off than he was. When he became an earl, after his father died, Effie was well quoted as saying: 'All I inherited was my title and my Coronation robes.' We paid him well to act as the club's 'greeter' and just to be seen around the place. We thought he would appeal to the sort of people who would use the club. I liked Effie and we treated him with respect. It's not true that I used to take the piss out of him by saying things like 'Get the effing tea, Effie.'

Esmerelda's Barn didn't work out for us, really, because of the tax men. They were getting upset because we weren't paying any, and they started to put a lot of pressure on us. It was them who forced us to cut our losses and get out of the West End. They were getting really heavy and we were mindful of the fact that it was the Revenue who put Al Capone out of business. It was a pity. We enjoyed watching the hooray Henrys getting their comeuppance at the card tables and the roulette wheels. But in the end we decided the whole deal was costing us too much and giving us too much hassle.

Sexually, too, the sixties was a good time. It was a time of real freedom. I have never made any secret that I am bisexual. I like men as well as women. I don't think there is anything wrong in that. Some people have criticized me for it, over the years, but the ones I have heard making comments have lived to regret it. I have even been open enough to explain my feelings on this to *Scene Out*, which is a magazine for gays.

I first knew when I was fifteen that I felt attracted to other boys. That was when I first had sex with one. I can't remember much about it now. I did tell my mum and dad, though, and they said it made no difference to them. My first real love was a young Jewish boy, Willy, who lived over the road from us. I fancied him and he knew it. He was beautiful, really handsome, but I never got in there, though I'd like to have done. I was in love with two boys when I was at Parkhurst prison, Peter and Lou. I had a tattoo done with Pete's name on it. When I was younger, in London, I had lots of relationships. I didn't go to gay bars, though, and places like that. In any case, there weren't many of them then. I enjoyed going to parties and hotel dos instead. London in the sixties was good, lots of nice, beautiful boys. The boys in Tangiers were also particularly beautiful. I've mixed with people from all walks of life and I have told them about my sexuality. If they don't like it, that's tough on them. If they are phoney friends, they won't want to know. Some people didn't like it, but I took no notice. If you hide it, it makes you feel bad. It makes you ill.

A young gay, from Germany, wrote to me about his sexuality and asked me how he should adapt, and what his friends would think. I told him not to worry about his friends; if they are true friends it will make no difference, if they are not, well, he doesn't need them anyway. Many great men have been either homosexual or bisexual. Gordon of Khartoum, Lawrence of Arabia. People in all walks of life are gay, boxers, sportsmen, politicians, actors, artists, some of the most talented people in the world. People can be more open about it now. They didn't dare so much in the fifties and sixties. I have slept with a lot of men, both famous and not famous, but I would never name any of them. Of course, in prisons and special hospitals like Broadmoor there is a lot of homosexual things going on. These days you have to be careful because of Aids, but before I married Kate I got them to test me for HIV because I thought it was only fair to her. I am pleased to say the test was negative.

Like I said, the early to middle sixties was good for me and Reg. In 1964 we moved into two luxury flats at Cedra Court, Cazenove Road, in Clapton. We did them up nicely. Mine had a big tank full of tropical fish in the lounge and I slept in a four-poster bed. Our clothes came from Woods, in East London, and we always wore the most expensive suits, shirts and shoes that you could buy. We both drove Mercedes cars and we ate and drank like lords. But, as I've said, we also gave a lot of money away. I'm not boasting about it, it's just a fact.

We always knew the police were watching us, trying to spot what we were up to, and we got into a bit of bother in 1965. The police did us for demanding money with menaces from a feller called Hew McCowan, who was the son of a Scottish baronet. McCowan ran a club called the Hideaway, in Gerrard Street, and he claimed we had demanded protection money from him. He said we had threatened to hurt him and damage his club if he didn't pay us. The truth was, he owed us money and we were trying to get it back. They also did me for possession of a knife. They sent us to Brixton prison to await the trial and they kept us waiting there for weeks. It was outrageous. So Lord Boothby, a friend of ours, stood up in the House of Lords and asked Her Majesty's Government 'whether it is their intention to keep the Kray brothers in prison for an indefinite period without trial'.

His remarks caused a sensation in the Press, but we were very grateful to him for his help. Lord Boothby was a friend, nothing more than that. We met him socially and there was nothing sexual between him and me. Soon after his comments we were released and, on 15 April 1965, we were cleared of all charges. We went straight home to Vallance Road and had one of the biggest parties the East End has ever seen. Twenty-five days later we got our revenge. Through a third party we bought the Hideaway off McCowan – and changed its name to the El Morocco. He was upset when he found out, but we thought it served him and the police right for trying to stitch us. By this time everybody knew about the Krays. We were getting more publicity than the Beatles. After we were cleared we had many letters and telegrams, including one from Judy Garland. The police wouldn't let it rest, though, and they even claimed the jury in the McCowan trial had been 'got at' by us. Was it true? No, but I agree with Reg, who spoke about this in his book, *Born Fighter*. If a man finds himself in the dock when totally innocent, then discovers that perjured evidence was being used against him by the police, and realizes that the only way out is for him to corrupt a jury, what would he do? Would he do so through friends? Or would he just sit there and suffer the consequences of a long jail sentence, passed on him because of fabricated evidence? As Reg says, on more than one occasion when we have found ourselves faced with this moral dilemma we have acted in accordance with the will to survive, and we have corrupted some members of a particular jury. We have known this to happen in many criminal trials over the years, where friends of ours have been fitted up by the police. If you think this is bad, ask yourself what you would do if you found yourself wrongly in the dock, and if you had the means to corrupt and sway the jury and walk to freedom. As Reg says, and it is true, crooked police officers – and there are a few, namely detectives – are treacherous. Most uniformed police are all right; they are basically straight and do a difficult job for poor pay. In the sixties, of course, jury-fixing was much easier. Nowadays, verdicts are decided by a majority of jurors whereas then if one member of a jury disagreed with the others there would have to be a retrial. So it was obviously much easier then to get at one member of the jury, or maybe two to be on the safe side. Jury-fixing, though, could be a very expensive business. It cost us a lot of money.

Four days after our acquittal on the McCowan charge Reg

got married. His bride was a beautiful twenty-one-year-old East End girl called Frances Shea, who'd been a childhood sweetheart. They married on 19 April 1965, at St James the Great church in Bethnal Green, and the service was conducted by the Reverend Albert Foster, who had been a character witness for us in the McCowan trial at the Old Bailey. I was the best man, David Bailey took the wedding photos and many famous names in sport and show-business were there. So were hundreds of well-wishers. It was a fantastic day. Tragically, only two years later Frances was dead. She had been quite ill and suffered a nervous breakdown. Her death was a terrible blow to us all, especially Reg, of course, and it was many months before he was able to come to terms with it. He loved Frances very much and there has never been another woman in his life.

Meanwhile, my friendship with Lord Boothby was making headlines again. The *Sunday Mirror* wrote a story about 'a top-level Scotland Yard investigation into the alleged homosexual relationship between a prominent peer and a leading thug in the London underworld'. Boothby sued them and won forty thousand pounds. The newspaper claimed that an investigation had been ordered by the Metropolitan Police Chief Commissioner, Sir Joseph Simpson. The article also spoke of 'parties in Mayfair attended by the peer and the thug', of visits to Brighton with 'other prominent public men', and of 'a relationship' between the peer, an East End gangster and some clergymen. There were also allegations of blackmail. There was such a stink in the press that the Home Secretary, Henry Brooke, made a statement about it.

Eventually IPC Ltd, the owners of the *Sunday Mirror*, apologized to Lord Boothby and paid him damages, and their chairman, Cecil King, issued a statement in which he said: 'I am satisfied that any imputation of an improper nature against Lord Boothby is completely unjustified.' There was no apology or damages for me, despite all the publicity which we could have done without. The only good thing about it, as far as I was concerned was that people now knew about my bisexuality. I didn't have to try and hide my leanings any more. But I still say there was nothing sexual between me and Lord Boothby. Apart from anything else, he wasn't my type.

After all that, things weren't going too bad for me and Reg until one night in March 1966, and a tragedy which had nothing to do with us. Up until that time we'd sort of shared control of London's underworld with the Richardson gang, south of the river. Charlie Richardson and his brother Eddie controlled south London. They were scrap-metal dealers who had other interests on the side. Their two top men were Frankie Fraser, who was known as Mad Frankie, and George Cornell. The Richardson gang was respected by some people and feared by others. We got on with them okay until Cornell started to mix it, stirring up trouble between us. No one liked George Cornell. He was a trouble-maker and a drunk and he liked to hurt people, especially people who couldn't defend themselves. He liked to torture old tramps and people like that. He was a bully, and enjoyed cruelty and pain. The Richardsons and Frankie Fraser eventually carried the can for much of what he did. We got on okay with Frankie Fraser and he later became a very good friend to us. But on this night in 'sixty-six, the Richardson gang went to a club called Mr Smith's, at Rushey Green, on the main road from London to Eastbourne at Catford. Later it was said that they expected to find us there as well, but we knew nothing about it. We did know the club, though. It was a drinking club, a nice place. But one member of our Firm was there, a close friend of ours called Richard Hart. A nice feller, about thirty, who had a lovely wife and young kids. A big fight started in the club and Richard Hart was shot to death. Everyone knew it was Cornell who shot him. Cornell had only gone there because he wanted a fight. But he was the one who got away, the others didn't. There was a big police hunt and a long trial and, at the end of it, Charlie Richardson got twenty-five years on various charges, Eddie Richardson got fifteen years, and Frankie Fraser got ten years.

The papers called it 'The Torture Trial', because a lot of evidence was given by men who claimed they'd been tortured by the gang. Two other members of the gang, Roy Hall and Thomas Clark, also went down.

I don't know about the Richardsons being involved in torture trials and things like that, but I know that Cornell did that sort of thing. Charlie Richardson called me and Reg 'mugs' in his book, published in 1991, but if we were mugs, what does that make him? We kept going a lot longer than he did, and we would have been okay if we hadn't made a couple of mistakes. The problem with the Richardson business, and all the publicity, was that it put even more police pressure on us and, of course, Cornell was still free. He was always going to be a problem for us.

But me and Reg weren't thinking about that too much at the time. We were in the process of trying to set up some links with the Mafia in America. We were always looking to the future, and we thought that was the way to go. But getting into America was difficult because of our criminal records. They were a bit choosy about who they let in. Then I met an American feller by the name of Peter Wyant. He was known as a wheeler-dealer, a Mr Fix-it, and he seemed to have plenty of contacts.

He said to me one day: 'I hear you can't get a visa to go to the States. Well, I can get you there.' It was going to cost, of course. He took me to the American embassy in Paris and he seemed to know people there. He had a long talk with a woman, and eventually she said to me: 'I know you have got convictions, but you will be allowed to go to America for a few days on holiday. Everything will be fixed.' And it was. Eventually I flew to America with a friend of mine called Dickie Morgan. But when we landed at Kennedy Airport in New York a reception committee was waiting for us.

The FBI were there and they searched us. They found nothing but we were then taken to the embassy in New York.

After a lot of talking and questions we were told we could stay in America for just seven days. But we were told if we stepped out of line we would be thrown out immediately. Wyant took us to meet Joe Kaufman, an Italian-American Jew, who was to be our middle man, our contact with the Mafia. Kaufman was friendly and said he would set up a meet with Frank Ileano, one of the top men with the famous New York Mafia family, the Gallos. They were three brothers, Joe Gallo, also known as Crazy Joe, Larry, and Al, who was known as Kid Blast, because he would 'blow' people away as soon as look at them. I was excited by this. Kaufman took me to a house in President Street, in Brooklyn. We were told that Ileano was waiting for us in a private bar nearby.

When we finally met, Frank Ileano told me to sit down. But while I was sitting down his brother Armando, who was a tiny man known as the Dwarf, stood behind me with a weapon in his hand. I thought of the old saying, 'Mark well the man whom God has marked.' Frank Ileano asked me a lot of questions about our operation in London. Kaufman told him he could check me out with a gangster called Angelo Bruno, from Philadelphia, who had been to London and knew our set-up. Ileano said: 'Don't worry, I will.' He then left the room to go to a phone. When he came back he said: 'I've checked you out and Bruno says you're okay.' I was relieved. After that we had some coffee and spoke about doing a deal. The Americans were mainly interested in getting involved in gambling in London and other big cities like Birmingham and Manchester. They do that sort of thing in a big way. We were happy for them to do it, provided they counted us in. Ileano arranged for us to meet again that evening. He said he would show me round New York and I would meet some important people.

That night he took us to a club called the Mousetrap. Later, in another club, he gave me a note from Al Gallo. He said he was sorry he couldn't meet me in person, but I was 'hot'. He said the FBI had a tail on me and were watching where I went and who I met. He also said he thought we could do business. I was pleased because I thought I had made a good contact.

Frank Ileano then said to me: 'Come on now, relax, enjoy your time in the Big Apple.' And that's what I did. I saw it all, the Bowery, Chinatown and Little Italy. The only place I didn't go was Harlem because Martin Luther King had just been assassinated and it was considered too dangerous for a white man to go there. I was pleased as well to meet some of my boxing heroes. I met Lee Oma, who had fought Britain's Tony Woodcock, Tony Zale, a former world middleweight champion, and the great Rocky Graziano, another former world middleweight champion. Graziano was a big hero of mine. I was surprised to discover that he was a chain-smoker and drank a lot of Scotch. He was a very nice feller, though, and I spent a very pleasant evening with him in a steak bar called Gallaghers. The week passed quickly. I had a good time and I felt it had been useful for the future. In the end we never got things going with the Americans like we wanted, because of our own problems with the law, but we did do some business with them. It was a pity, it would have made us very powerful. But I did make some good contacts and some good friends, like Frank and Armando Ileano. I later gave Frank a diamond ring worth a thousand pounds.

Another good contact I made was a Sicilian-American called Eddie Pucci, who was a close friend of Frank Sinatra. Later I used to meet with Pucci at the Hilton Hotel in London, and when we were talking in his room he always played the radio really loud, in case the room was bugged. Once he told me he liked Old English bull terriers, so I sent him one to America. Eddie was our contact with a Chicago gangster called Sam Giancano. Both of them were later gunned to death. Another good friend was Joe Pacano, claimed by the American press to be the top Mafia boss, who died from a massive stroke. He became one of my best friends and he sent me a gold cat's-eye ring with two big diamonds in it. I treasure this ring. I once made up a poem about Joe Pacano. I called it 'My Best Friend Joe'.

I returned to England quite happy and pleased. Soon after I got back some of our American friends put our loyalty to the test. They asked us if we would help Joe Louis, the great American boxer, who had fallen on hard times. Joe wanted to come to England for a holiday. We fixed it up and gave him a great time. I rang some good friends of ours, the Levy brothers who ran the Dolce Vita nightclub in Newcastle, and they agreed to pay Joe a thousand pounds to appear at their club. I met Joe at Gatwick airport and, with a friend called Mickey Morris, drove him up to Newcastle. While we were there me and Mickey and a good friend called Sammy Lederman went with Joe on board an American aircraft carrier which was in the port. The Yank sailors were as excited as we were to meet him. I liked Joe Louis, and me and Reg have warm feelings for the Levy brothers who later sent someone down with five thousand pounds to help with the costs of our court case. They were good friends at a time when good friends were hard to find.

By 1967 things were still going fine, though we knew about Scotland Yard's interest in us and, in particular, a detective called Leonard 'Nipper' Read. Our business interests were still doing okay, but we never learned one good lesson from the Americans, and that was this. In America, a Mafia boss doesn't kill his enemies himself, he gets someone else to do it. Me and Reg always did our own dirty business. And that was why, less than two years later, we were both locked away. The impossible had happened: the Krays had been got by the police. And all because we killed two men, Jack McVitie and George Cornell. And because we didn't realize how corrupt the legal system could be. And because we didn't realize we were surrounded by many traitors. Sir Joseph Simpson, the Home Office pathologist, said that McVitie and Cornell were such bad men that they wouldn't be missed. Maybe. But they've still cost us half of our lives.

CHAPTER THREE

The Killings

I never killed George Cornell because he called me a fat poof. That's all lies, rubbish. No, if Cornell had called me a fat poof I would have killed him there and then. No messing. I killed Cornell in the Blind Beggar public house because I had a pact, an agreement, with some other people, influential people, that if Cornell and the gang he was with – the Richardsons, south of the river – if they started a war, I would do something about it.

Well, they did start a war. There was a battle at Mr Smith's club, which was started by the Richardsons and Cornell. A very good friend of ours called Richard Hart got killed in the fight, yet he was just an innocent bystander. The Richardsons got done for that, but Cornell got away.

So I kept to my word. Even though others didn't, I still kept to the pact. I went and done Cornell. I got a message that he was involved in the business at Mr Smith's, I got a message asking if I would keep my word. When I give my word, I keep it. I never thought about the police, I just done it. Cornell deserved it. He was a flash, arrogant bastard. He was a bully.

People often describe me as a cold-blooded killer and Cornell as the innocent, unarmed victim. That's a load of rubbish. Cornell was a hard man, a very hard man. And he was nasty with it. But what people don't realize is that Cornell was also a killer. On his own admission, to me personally, he killed a man called Thomas 'Ginger' Marks.

Marks was a car dealer. Just after midnight, one morning in January 1965, he was shot dead when he was walking with a mate of his called George Evans in Cheshire Street, in Bethnal Green. According to Evans a car drove up alongside them, slowed down, and a voice called out, 'Ginge'. Marks turned round and a shot rang out. Evans got in a panic and ran round the corner and dived under a parked lorry. He says the car drove off and he went back to the spot where he and Marks had been walking, but there was no sign of Ginger. When the police came they found blood on the pavement, a bullet hole in the wall and a used cartridge, plus the black, horn-rimmed glasses which Marks always wore. But there was no sign of Ginger.

The police searched everywhere for him and the newspapers called it 'The Case of the Phantom Shooting' because no one could find Marks's body. They reckoned that he had been shot in the stomach, because the bullet hole was only a few feet off the ground. But no one turned up at any London hospital or doctor's surgery with a shotgun wound in the stomach. One of the newspapers offered a reward of five thousand pounds for information. I could have told them that Marks was dead – and that George Cornell had killed him.

How do I know? Because George Cornell told me himself before he and I fell out. Some time before Marks got done, he and Cornell had a big row. I acted as the peacemaker and got 'em both together in the Grave Maurice pub in Whitechapel. We had a few drinks and sorted out the bit of business that was causing the problem between them and they shook hands. But when Marks left the pub, Cornell started mouthing off again, as usual, and he said he hated Marks and one day he would 'blow his head off'. I think, really, that Cornell was a bit scared of Marks and he knew that Marks always carried a gun and he would use it if he had to.

After Marks was done, and no one knew what had happened to him, Cornell told me that he had 'pulled the trigger' on him. He boasted about it quite openly. He never told me what he had done with the body and I never asked him. In our business you mind your own business. But getting rid of a body wasn't a problem. So when I killed Cornell, later, I was only killing a killer.

Of course, Leonard 'Nipper' Read don't see it that way. Read, the policeman who claims the credit for doing me and Reg and who's made money out of doing me and Reg down, tries to blame us for killing Ginger Marks. Or at least a member of our Firm. And in his book about his life, Read says Marks wasn't the target at all. He claims the real target was the man who was walking with Marks on the night he got shot – George Evans.

Read says:

> Apparently a friend of the Firm had been shot by a man who discovered his victim had been having an affair with his wife. The victim had sought revenge and a plan had been hatched to kill this attacker. Watch had been kept but, unfortunately, the retribution was handed out to the wrong man. The proposed victim was walking along Cheshire Street together with a man called Ginger Marks, when a car drew up alongside them and someone called out. Marks must have thought he heard his nickname, 'Ginge', and stepped forward, only to be shot and killed. The body was bundled into the car and driven off. When the mistake was discovered the contract was renewed.

And what is Read's evidence to link me and Reg to this murder? A photograph of the intended victim which was given to the killer to help him identify his victim. That photograph, showing the target's face, had been cut out of a much bigger photograph. And that bigger photograph, Read says, was later found – minus the face which had been cut out of it – amongst the property of me and Reg when we were arrested.

That evidence is pitiful. If we'd done Ginger Marks I would hold up my hands and say so.

I never made any secret about doing Cornell. I'd known Cornell since I was a kid. He was from Watney Street in the East End. We knew him but we were never what you'd call friends. That didn't stop us helping him out when he was a bit older, when he came out of the nick and he never had a bob to his name. We gave him a few quid and got him fixed up with some decent clothes. But that never made any difference. There was always a bit of a problem, he was that kind of feller. Eventually he moved south of the river and joined up with the Richardsons. He was always a vicious bastard but I was never frightened of him or his older brother, Jimmy, who had a badly scarred face after he got slashed.

Cornell was under six foot tall, but he was a powerful feller with a big, thick neck. When we had our problem he was only in his mid-thirties but he looked a lot older. He had a sort of curled lip which always made it look like he was sneering at you. He liked violence. Like I said, he used to take old tramps down to a cellar and torture them. I don't know about the Richardsons torturing people. I don't know about that, but I know that Cornell did. He enjoyed it. He once got three years for slashing a woman's face. He was a lippy bastard. When me and Reg were in Brixton on a menaces charge, he told a friend of ours, 'The King is dead.' This was a deliberate insult to me. It was Cornell saying he hoped they would put me inside. It was not a good thing to say, it was out of order.

Maybe things would have been okay. But then there was the business at Mr Smith's, when our friend Richard Hart got shot dead. Richard Hart was a real nice feller, a good friend. He wasn't a gangster or anything like that, and he had a nice wife and two young kids. He never deserved to get it, and it shouldn't have happened at a place like Mr Smith's. It was a nice club, it wasn't a rough place. After Richard Hart was shot the Richardsons were soon arrested, so was Frankie Fraser. That was fair enough, they'd all been involved. But somehow Cornell never got picked up for it, or if he was he must have had a good alibi.

Anyway, a few days later, Cornell turns up again right out of the blue. I can remember the date as if it was yesterday – 6 March 1966. I'm having a drink in a pub called the Lion in Tapp Street. This pub was also called the Widow's, or Madge's, because it was run by a widow called Madge. There was a few of us there drinking, me, Reg, Ian Barrie, John 'Scotch Jack' Dickson, and some others. Then I got a phone call. I had already had a message that Cornell had been involved at Mr Smith's. Like I said, I had given my word that I would deal with Cornell. This phone call tells me that Cornell is drinking at a pub called the Blind Beggar, which is right in the middle of our manor and less than half a mile away from where we were all sat drinking. I told Ian Barrie to come with me and I told John Dickson to get a car, and to drive us to the Beggar's.

It's funny, really, I read one of them London tourist guides which someone gave me, the other day, and it talks about the Beggar's in there. It said: 'The newly renovated Blind Beggar gained notoriety when Ronnie Kray and an accomplice murdered George Cornell as he sat drinking there. The pub's atmosphere has changed dramatically now and, with a pleasant garden for children, it has become, like so many other East End pubs, a place for the entire family.'

It must have changed a hell of a lot! In 1966 it was nothing like that. It was a depressing place; it had a flat front and two long bars which curved in a short of U-shape and joined up the back, in the rear snug. That's all there was to it, the public bar on the right, the saloon bar on the left and the snug at the end. And the landlord's accommodation was upstairs above the bars. The place wasn't smartly done out or anything like that, and it always seemed sort of dark in there. It was a depressing pub.

The only interesting thing about it was its name, which was based on an East End play, four hundred years old, called *The Blind Beggar of Bethnal Green*.

It's part of East End folklore, the story of Bessee, the daughter of a blind beggar, who was being courted by four rich men – a knight, a businessman, an innkeeper's son and an aristocrat. They all wanted to marry her, until they learned her father was a beggar. Then they lost interest, all except the knight, who went to her father and asked if he could marry her. Then Bessee's father, who everyone thought was a beggar, surprised everyone by giving her a hundred pounds for her wedding gown, which was like thousands in them days, and a dowry of three thousand pounds, which was like a small fortune. Then, at the end of the story, at the wedding feast, the blind beggar reveals that he is the son of Simon de Montfort, who founded England's parliament. Everyone thought he had died in the battle of Evesham but, in fact, he had only lost his sight. His life was saved by a lady who later bore him a child who was, of course, the beautiful Bessee of Bethnal Green. And she and the knight, so they say, lived happily ever after.

Like I said, I intended to kill Cornell that night. I had to. It was as simple as that.

Dickson drove me and Ian Barrie to the Beggar's, in one of the Firm's cars, a Ford Cortina. When we arrived I told him to wait outside while me and Ian Barrie went inside to see if Cornell was there. We went into the saloon bar and he was there all right, talking to two other fellers. He was sat on a stool drinking a glass of light ale. They were the only ones in the bar apart from the barmaid. There was a record on the juke box which was very popular at the time called 'The Sun Ain't Gonna Shine Anymore', by an American group called The Walker Brothers.

As we walked in Cornell looked up and said, in that sneering way he had, 'Well, look who's here . . .'

I took a 9 mm Mauser pistol out of my pocket and Ian Barrie took out a .32 revolver. I was quite calm. Cornell was still sneering. I shot him. The bullet went into his forehead, just above his right eye. It went straight through his head. He fell off his stool. He just fell forward and I knew he was dead. I see blood come on his forehead and he just fell forward. I knew he was dead and I was pleased. They said in court that Ian Barrie fired a couple of shots into the ceiling. I don't know about that, I can't remember. I do remember that the needle on the juke box got stuck on the record and it kept on repeating the words 'The sun ain't gonna shine anymore . . . anymore . . . anymore . . .'

Nothing was said. Cornell's pals had disappeared, there was no sign of the barmaid. Me and Ian Barrie just walked out of the pub, got in the car and Dickson drove us back to the Lion. I had a chat with Reg. I knew I had to get rid of my clothes and the gun and have a good scrub, so we went to the Chequers at Walthamstow, which was about six miles from the Lion. This was one of the places where we kept a change of clothing.

We went upstairs to listen to the BBC news on the landlord's radio. We had a few drinks and eventually it came on. The announcer said something like: 'A man has been shot in an East End public house. He was later identified as Mr George Cornell of Camberwell Green. After the shooting he was taken to the Maida Vale Hospital, but was found to be dead on arrival.'

Like I said, I was pleased. He was scum. I have never had one regret about killing Cornell. I was sorry for his family, of course I was, but if it hadn't been Cornell it would have been me. I had kept my word; I always keep my word.

I knew there had been witnesses in the Beggar's. But someone had a word with the people who had been there, including the barmaid and an old feller who'd been in the public bar. See, if we'd really been the bad bastards some people have said we are, then we'd have made sure that barmaid kept her mouth permanently shut. That's what Cornell would have done. But I can honestly say we were never like that. We never hurt women or children, and the only men we hurt were those stupid enough to get in our way.

A few days after I killed Cornell we were at a party at a flat in Lea Bridge Road, in Leyton, when the police came barging in and arrested us. We'd been expecting them, of course. In fact, we were surprised it had taken them so long. Chief Inspector Tommy Butler, the head of Scotland Yard's Flying Squad, was in charge of them. Butler was the man who later tried to track down the Great Train Robbers – and a right balls-up he made of most of that. Me and Reg was put in an identity parade and we saw the blonde barmaid from the Beggar's walking towards us. But she walked straight by and never picked us out. Tommy Butler was well pissed off.

Like I say, I always intended to kill George Cornell. But the killing of Jack McVitie was different. Sure, we killed him and we got done for it, but there was never, like, a definite plan to kill McVitie. It just sort of happened. As a matter of fact, Reggie should never have been done for the murder of McVitie, it should have been self-defence, and I'll tell you why. McVitie's real name was John, but everyone called him Jack. He was known as Jack the Hat because he always wore a hat to hide his bald head. He was very vain about his appearance and no one ever saw him without his hat. He wore it if he came to the front door to answer it. They say he even wore it in the bath. He wasn't on our Firm, but he used to do odd jobs for us. He was quite tough, he had very big forearms, and he liked to think he was a hard man. His big problem was he liked to drink a lot, but he couldn't hold his drink. He got nasty.

McVitie started to let us down. He went into the 211 club in Balham High Road, which was owned by our friend Freddie Foreman. McVitie was drunk, so Freddie told him to leave. He did, but then he came back again, and he caused a scene and did some damage. It was silly. He upset another friend of ours, Ron Olives, in a club called the Log Cabin, in Wardour Street, whch the boxer Billy Walker had an interest in, with his brother George. Then he misbehaved himself in our club, the Regency. He took a gun out and fired a couple of shots at a feller called

Tommy Flanagan. Thank Christ he missed. Then he cut a feller with a knife in the basement, walked upstairs and wiped off the blood on his knife on the dress of a woman who was having a drink at the bar.

We weren't looking for trouble with McVitie, but he never listened when you gave him advice. He did us out of some money and then he went down the Regency Club and threatened John Barry with a gun. Barry had an interest in the club with us. That was in October 1967.

McVitie was waving a shotgun around, a sawn-off shotgun, and saying things about me. Making threats. Reggie talked to him about it in a Chinese restaurant, but McVitie never paid any attention. He was silly. That turned out to be his last supper. Me and Reg spoke about it and we decided we would sort McVitie out.

We set up a little drinks party at a flat in Evering Road, Stoke Newington. It belonged to a friend of ours. Everybody called her Blonde Carol. That was on the night of the 28th. Me and Reg was there, with the Lambrianous, Chris and Tony, and Ron Bender, who was on the Firm. There was a couple of other fellers there, young friends of mine. We'd had a few drinks, gin and tonic, and we got a call telling us that McVitie had turned up again at the Regency. I told Tony Lambrianou to go and fetch him. Tell him there was a party on, there was some drinks and some women. We knew Jack would come.

I knew Reggie had a gun with him. But you had to have a weapon with you if you were going to get involved with someone like McVitie. Like, no one had said, right, Reg, take a gun and you can shoot McVitie. It wasn't like that.

Everyone knew that McVitie was going to get a beating. Reggie wasn't the only one who was tooled up. Anyway, eventually Tony Lambrianou turns up with McVitie, but there was two other men as well, friends of McVitie. They were two brothers, Ray and Alan Mills. Ronnie Hart, our cousin, had come as well. McVitie was surprised to see us and we told him to sit in a chair.

We told the Mills brothers to bugger off and forget what they had seen. Reggie said to McVitie: 'We warned you more than once about causing trouble for us, but you never listened. I told you about the trouble you had at Fred's club [the 211].'

Then Jack did a silly thing. He said to Reg: 'Fred's club has got nothing to do with you.'

That made Reggie mad. He took out his gun, a Beretta, and tried to shoot McVitie. He pulled the trigger, there was a click, but the gun never fired. It was jammed. Then McVitie jumped up and attacked Reggie with a knife. He went for him with the knife, but Reg got it off him. Then he done him with the knife. So it should have been self-defence. Reggie did him three times with the knife, twice in his body and once in his face. All that stuff about McVitie running across the room and trying to dive through a window, all that is rubbish. There wasn't time. It happened too quick. It always does. McVitie was on the floor, there was a lot of blood. Ron Bender bent down, listened to his heart, and said, 'He's dead.'

That's what happened. He went for Reggie and Reggie done him in self-defence. But all that never came out, all the grasses said that Reg done him and McVitie just sat there and took it.

Those rats the Mills brothers, they grassed us. And they weren't even there. McVitie deserved it, he was a bad man. He once broke a woman's back by throwing her out of a car. We had to deal with him, he'd been telling other people he was going to shoot Reggie.

They've never found Jack the Hat's body. People like Tony Lambrianou may say they know how we got rid of him. But they don't. Only me and Reggie know, but we won't tell. We never grass, we never have.

But, believe me, just like Cornell, Jack McVitie wasn't a nice man. Even Lambrianou wrote in a newspaper: 'He [McVitie] wasn't the meek little man portrayed in the film, *The Krays*. He was a known heavy man, an active robber, capable of anything.

If Jack the Hat was going to die, that is how he would have wanted to go. Reggie didn't do society such a bad turn.'

That is right. We only handed out punishment when it was deserved. One feller called me a fat slob, so I had to do him. We were in a pub at the time, so I went to the toilet and told someone to pass a message to him that I wanted a quiet word, in private. As he came into the toilet I slashed him with a knife. He had to have plastic surgery.

Another time, a man came to see me – like, I mean a man who was straight, who had no criminal connections, but who knew that the Krays could help him where the police weren't bothered – and he told me that a feller from Mile End had broken his daughter's nose in three places because she wouldn't have sex with him. The police didn't want to know. One of them told this man that his daughter was probably just a prick-teaser. Nice, eh? Just the sort of thing you want to hear if your daughter has been marked for life by some tearaway. Anyway, we knew of this feller that the man was complaining about, because we knew he had also broken the jaw of a seventeen-year-old boy in another unprovoked attack.

It was time something was done about him before he started getting ideas above his station. So I phoned this feller up and told him I wanted to meet him at Esmerelda's Barn. He fell for it; he thought because it was me calling him he was going to be given a job to earn himself some money. But he was a dirty little rat, so I thought I'd set an example with him for the whole East End. And I did. I taught him the lesson he would never forget with the hot poker. If he's alive today, then he'll still have the scars.

We've both been violent in our time, me and Reg, but neither of us ever actually enjoyed the violence. It's just like soldiers in the war, the SAS and all that. They're not violent people in themselves, really, but it's a job, and they have to do it. We were the same.

In the film *The Krays* they said we said we could get anything by fear, but we never said that. On the front cover of the video of the film it says: 'If people are afraid of you, you can do anything . . . remember that.' But we didn't operate like that. We used respect, not fear. There is a big difference. If people respect you they will do what you ask. If they are frightened of you they will simply run away and hide from you. People like Cornell and McVitie tried to rule people with fear. If you don't belive me, get hold of a book by Sir Joseph Simpson, the Home Office patholo-gist, who writes about Cornell and Jack the Hat and says they won't be missed and they was horrible people. We understood about people like them and we dealt with them. But what we could never understand was fellers like Ronnie Hart, our own cousin. Me and Reg had been really good to him, given him the good life, and yet – to save his own skin – he told Nipper Read everything he wanted to hear. He even made a statement implicating the two totally innocent friends of mine who had been at Blonde Carol's flat on the night Jack McVitie got it. Those two young fellers had to stand up to some very harsh police interroga-tion. But they refused to make statements. They acted like real men and I was very sorry when one of them later took an overdose of drugs, and died. I still feel Ronnie Hart acted very badly. I hope his family and friends realize what a little rat he is.

John Dickson was another. Dickson used to drive Reggie around. We gave him a job on the Firm when he came down from Scotland. He was skint till we gave him a chance. But he's another one who was willing to drop us in the shit just so's he would come up smelling of roses. And the snivelling little bastard has even cashed in and wrote a book about us.

He says in his book that after the disappearance of the Mad Axeman, Frank Mitchell, he stayed with me at my flat in Cedra Court. He wrote: 'I eventually dozed off. I was awakened by the smell of gas. The gas fire in my room had been left with the gas switch open. I got up and turned it off. I didn't sleep after that. My mind was working overtime. Did Ronnie come in and turn it on? Or did I, accidentally, turn it on? I never found the answer to that one.' But if I had really wanted to kill him, I would have done so straight out. And they would never have found his body in a million years.

The police and many others have tried to blame us for the death of Frank Mitchell, the Mad Axeman, in 1966. The truth of the matter is, me and Reg know who killed Frank Mitchell – and it wasn't us. We would never have killed Big Frank. We had too much admiration for him. For those who don't know it, let me tell you the story of one of the gamest men who ever worked in the underworld.

Frank Mitchell came from a large, poor family in Canning Town. He was a simple man, but a good man, and he was the biggest, strongest man I ever saw in my life. Right from an early age he was in and out of prisons and mental hospitals and they all tried, and failed, to break him. He was birched, given the cat-o'-nine-tails, even beaten to a pulp while he was strapped in a strait-jacket. But they never broke him. He escaped from Rampton and he escaped from Broadmoor by using the springs of his bed and turning them into a sort of key. When he was out he got into the house of a couple living nearby and he nearly frightened them to death by making them sit and have a cup of tea and watch the television with him. The problem was, he had an axe balanced on his knee at the time. That was how he got the name the Mad Axeman.

But he wasn't mad, Frank wasn't. And he wouldn't have hurt that couple. He only hurt people who got in his way, especially screws, in prison. Finally, they sent him to Dartmoor in Devon, which, at the time, they said was a prison that no one would ever escape from. Frank was there for nine years and the staff left him alone to do more or less what he wanted. They realized it was safer from their point of view because he could be a bit dangerous if he got angry. He had a hell of a life inside Dartmoor. When it all came out in court later, no one could believe it. Even the judge said, 'It all sounds like Cloud Cuckoo Land to me!'

Frank and his best friend in Dartmoor, another convict called Frank Benson, would wander in and out of the prison more or less as they wanted. They used to go riding on ponies across the moor, sometimes they would ride motorbikes they kept hidden near the prison, and sometimes they would go drinking in pubs on the moor. Frank even used to have sex with a local woman in a barn. Once he and Frank Benson – who was a small, quiet feller who knew how to handle Frank – took a taxi into Okehampton, the nearest town of any size, to buy a budgerigar. As long as the two Franks were back inside their cells by lights-out, none of the screws seemed to worry.

Dartmoor was a joke. Once my brother Reg disguised himself, used a false name, and went to visit Frank at the prison with the former boxer, Ted 'Kid' Lewis, to show some boxing films while Ted talked about his career to the cons. Reg even had dinner with the Governor after the event, and the Governor told him: 'Don't forget to come back again!'

Eventually Frank got fed up with Dartmoor and upset because the authorities wouldn't review his case. He asked us to get him away from the prison, so we did. On the 12 December 1966, we had him picked up by a car near the prison. Frank was with a working party and he just quietly walked away. By the time the stupid bastards realized he was gone, he was two hundred-odd miles away in London. We put him up at a flat in Barking owned by a friend of ours called Lennie Dunn.

Frank needed company, so some fellers in the Firm used to take it in turns to sit with him and chat to him. Mainly it was Scotch Jack Dickson, a feller called Billy Exley, and 'Mad' Teddy Smith. Smith wrote a letter for Frank Mitchell to the Home Secretary, asking that his case should be investigated, and his request for freedom should be considered. We sent copies of the letter to the *Daily Mirror* and *The Times*. We never got a reply from the Home Secretary.

Frank started to get restless and we didn't know what to do with him. We couldn't really pack him off back to Dartmoor, could we? Then Billy Exley and three Greek fellers said that, if we gave them some money, they'd get him a false passport and take him abroad. We weren't too happy, but Frank said it was what he wanted to do. So, on 23 December they took him away. I had bad feelings about it. Later we heard that Frank had fallen out with Exley and the Greeks. So they killed him. I was told it took three bullets to kill him, and that Exley pulled the trigger on the final shot, which went straight through Frank Mitchell's head. It was obvious to me that, once they'd got Frank away from us, they suddenly began to realize it was a bigger job than they thought. So they took the easy way out: they killed the big feller. So it was Exley and the Greeks who done him – not us.

But then Exley talked to Nipper Read, naming members of our Firm as the killers, and the bastard got away scot-free. At our trial the prosecution even told the court that Exley was a dying man with a bad heart who could go at any second. In fact, Billy's heart held out for another twenty years!

The whole thing was a non-starter. Albert Donaghue, a member of the Firm we had really trusted, told the court that 'it took eleven or twelve bullets to kill Frank Mitchell. I saw Freddie Foreman pump him full of bullets in a van in Barking.' Donaghue also claimed we gave Freddie Foreman a thousand pounds for killing Frank – and he said he heard another man, Alfred Gerrard, say: 'The bastard's still alive. Give him another one, Fred.' And that Jack Dickson said he'd heard three shots. And he claimed that I said to him: 'He's fucking dead. We had to get rid of him, he would have got us all into trouble.'

In the end, no one was convicted of killing Frank Mitchell. Now no one ever will be. Because the feller who did it, Billy Exley, is dead himself. And the Greek fellers who did it with him are long gone. But Frank Mitchell *is* dead, I don't doubt it. And, unfortunately for me and Reg, dead men can't talk.

CHAPTER FOUR

The Party's Over . . .

The beginning of the end for me and Reg probably started at Christmas 1967. We had a good Christmas but we didn't realize that Nipper Read had been to see Billy Exley. Read was a superintendent working from the Murder Squad at the Yard. We knew about him but we never thought he was anything special. We still don't.

Exley, the man he saw, was an ex-boxer who did odd jobs for us. He wasn't an important member of the Firm, but he knew bits and pieces. We know now that he and Read met at Exley's little flat in Woodseer Street, in the East End although Exley wouldn't come clean till later. In his book Read said: 'Once Billy Exley began to talk to me, so many pieces of the jigsaw began to fall into place and I learned that Jack "the Hat" McVitie and Billy Exley were sent to shoot Payne.'

During the first four months of 1968, Read and the policemen working with him – Frank Cater, Harry Mooney, Algie Hemmingway and Alan Wright – got at Liza, the nightclub hostess we'd paid to keep Frank Mitchell company at Lennie

Dunn's flat. She grassed and so did Dunn. Then they talked to the barmaid at the Blind Beggar and she named me as the man who shot George Cornell. It was all wrong. She didn't pick me out at the identification parade after Cornell was shot. She walked straight past me. But she picked me out in the trial at the Old Bailey. That can't be right. What's the point of identification parades in the first place? If a witness can't pick you out then, how can the same witness suddenly point you out in court months, years, later? I tried to say that in court, to say how unfair, how biased it was. But they whitewashed it all.

They finally came for us on 8 May 1968. It's funny, really, because after all the bad times I'd been through with my mental problems, I'd been starting to feel a lot better, much more like my old self. And Reg was in good form too. The night they came for us had been the kind of night we always enjoyed. A few drinks at the pub with some of the Firm, then up the West End for some action at the clubs. We went to the Astor Club, off Berkeley Square, and we sat there drinking and talking till the early hours. We never thought anything was up. We knew there were some plain-clothes detectives in the club, we could always spot them a mile off, but that was nothing unusual. They were always following us about. Me and Reg eventually left the Astor and drove back to a flat we owned at Braithwaite House, in Old Street. He was with a girl, I had a feller with me. We all had a nightcap and went to bed.

We were all sound asleep when there was a hell of a commotion. I woke up to find my bed surrounded by police, some of them armed. They were led by Nipper Read and they'd smashed down the front door to get in. I noticed they were carrying .45 calibre Webley pistols and one of them was holding an iron bar. Read said to me: 'You are under arrest. Get out of bed with your hands in the air.' I was stark naked but that made no difference to them. Reg was brought into the room and Read said we were being charged with murder and other offences. He asked us if we'd got anything to say, and Reg said: 'Yes, Mr

Read. We've been expecting a frame-up for a long time, but we've got plenty of witnesses. There's a lot of people wanting to help us.'

At the time we believed that. We knew we had a bit of trouble here but we didn't think it was anything we couldn't handle. We'd been pulled in before and managed to sort it out. What we didn't realize was that, while we were being arrested, squads of armed police were smashing down other doors all over the East End and pulling in anyone they could find. There was something like eighteen arrests that night, all carried out at the same moment. And all of those arrested were kept well apart, so that no one knew what was going on. They pulled in everyone that night except Scotch Jack Dickson and my right-hand man, Ian Barrie. They arrested Dickson a few hours later, and they picked up Barrie next day in a pub in the East End. We were all sent to different prisons and Read started to work on the weak ones, the liars, the traitors, the grasses. The ones he could do a deal with so they could save their own skins.

By the middle of June we were getting whispers that the grassing had started. In his book Read says:

I saw Cornelius Whitehead in the chapel at Wandsworth Prison on 22 June . . .

The next day it was back to Wandsworth Prison, in the evening, to visit Tommy Cowley, who also wanted to see me. He had been charged with two cases of conspiracy to murder and with harbouring Frank Mitchell . . .

Four days after that I had a message for Jock Ions that Scotch Jack Dickson had asked to see me. I saw him that evening in the chapel, in a meeting which lasted some twenty-five minutes, and ended with him saying: 'For Christ's sake, don't let anyone know that you've seen me. I'd be dead. You know that, being here.' What he did not know was that he had become only one of a number who had the same fears . . .

All through that long wet summer of 'sixty-eight, with me and Reg locked up in isolation, many members of our Firm turned Judas. Read would visit them in prison, using false names and often in disguise, and in the privacy of hospital rooms and chapels and toilets they would tell their stories. We knew that Albert Donaghue had had several sessions with Read, so had Dickson and Ronnie Hart, our cousin. Dickson was a disgrace. He even had the audacity to say in court: 'The murders have got to stop. If Ronnie Kray had not been charged with Cornell's murder there would have been two other murders that I know of that would have been committed.' He also said: 'Someone has got to have the guts to come forward to say their piece. You have got the three of them [me, Reg and our brother Charlie] in the dock, but I was not guilty.'

Dickson was a rat. There is no other word for him. Eventually the trial got under way, and every day was like a fucking carnival as the prisoners were driven in from Brixton, Wandsworth and other prisons. Me and Reg were driven in from Brixton, with a cavalcade of police and prison vehicles, flashing lights, wailing klaxons, armed police and commandos. Each day the route was changed, to avoid, they said, any attempt to hijack us. All the way in to the Old Bailey the route was lined with hundreds of people, many of them waving at us. No kidding, at times it was like the coronation. Or an execution.

There were many charges against us, some of them quite stupid. They were just chucking everything at us, knowing that some of it would have to stick. It was pathetic – more than that, it was corrupt. As long as they could put us away for as long as possible, that was all they cared about. They charged me and Ian Barrie with the murder of George Cornell in the Blind Beggar. Barrie was one of the few members of the Firm to stay loyal. Ian Barrie was a real man. He remained loyal to us despite the tremendous pressures put on him by the police. His fellow Scot, Dickson, stood up in court and said he thought Barrie was wrong to stand in the dock 'thinking it was big to be convicted with

Ronnie Kray about a murder which he had known nothing about previously, and in which he had no concern'.

Reg was charged with being an accessory to Cornell's murder. Both of us, with Tony and Chris Lambrianou, Ron Bender and Anthony Barry, the co-owner of the Regency club, were charged with the murder of Jack McVitie. Barry had not been present at the murder and was subsequently acquitted. He, too, gave evidence against us.

Me and Reg and Tommy Cowley – one of the first of the traitors to ask to see Nipper Read – and our old friend Dickie Morgan were also charged with conspiring to kill a Maltese feller, George Caruana, between January and May 1968. This shows the depths to which the police were sinking to make sure something stuck against the Krays. They said we hired a feller called Paul Elvey to kill Caruana because he was trying to muscle in on our business. They claimed Elvey would have used either a crossbow or an explosive device to kill Caruana. The whole thing was nonsense. Me and Reg and Cowley were also charged with conspiring to murder an unnamed man in 1967, again using Paul Elvey as the hit man, only this time Elvey was to use a hypodermic syringe filled with poison and built into a suitcase. The prosecution claimed that the syringe was designed to work when the case was swung against the body of the intended victim. Death would be instant but would take the appearance of a heart attack. I had never heard anything like it.

And the charges went on and on. I was charged with causing grievous bodily harm to a man at Esmerelda's Barn. (The prosecution alleged that after he had upset a friend of ours, I invited him to the club and then placed a red-hot poker on his face and shoulders.)

With Reg and our brother Charlie, I was charged with demanding money with menaces from two of our financial advisers who were now two of the prosecution's chief witnesses, but who had in their time swindled thousands out of me and Reg.

Me and Reg, with Connie Whitehead and Albert Donaghue,

were charged with murdering Frank Mitchell. We were also charged with aiding Mitchell's escape from Dartmoor. And there was a whole string of fraud charges as well. All in all, the police were determined they were going to get us on something! Defending us we had some top men: John Platts-Mills, QC, for me; Paul Wrightson, QC, for Reg; and Desmond Vowden, QC, for Charlie. On the opening day of the trial we got more media coverage than Earl Ray, the man who shot Martin Luther King and who had been arrested at London airport.

There were nine of us in the dock and Melford Stevenson started that nonsense about us wearing numbered cards around our necks. I soon told him to fuck off. The court was packed every day. In his book, *My Manor*, Charlie Richardson spoke sneeringly about 'the little grey people' who queued up to get into the court when he and his gang faced their torture trial charges. But ours was a more star-studded affair. We had plenty of star names watching us in court, including Charlton Heston. And tickets for the trial were changing hands for big money on the black market. Touts were even outside the Old Bailey buying and flogging tickets. But as the trial went on I realized we were in deep trouble.

One by one, trusted members of our Firm took their place in the witness box. I'll never forget Dickson and what he said. But it was when I saw the barmaid from the Beggar's that I knew it was all over. The barmaid, who they called Mrs X, was taken through her evidence by Kenneth Jones, QC. He got her to tell the jury how she was working in the Blind Beggar on the night Cornell was shot – and how she had witnessed the murder. Then came her big moment. Would she, asked Mr Jones, look around the court and point to the man she had seen shoot Cornell? Straight away she pointed at me.

'Number one, over there. Ronald Kray,' she said. As clear as that. And this was the woman who had failed to pick me out, face to face, in an identification parade. Shortly after, she picked out Ian Barrie as the man who was with me.

Nipper Read said later: 'It was at this moment I believed

justice was going to be done.' I didn't feel they played fair, using the barmaid the way they did. But I never felt violent or angry towards her. Funnily enough, I felt a bit sorry for her.

Later I had to give evidence. Read wrote about that: 'As he climbed the steps of the witness box, the jury had an even closer look at him. They must have noticed that he looked bigger than he did when he was seated in the dock. And they probably felt, as most people did, that he carried an air of menace with him.'

Mr Platts-Mills questioned me about the Cornell killing which, of course, I denied. I also told him the truth: a few days before Cornell was murdered, I had sent a box of chocolates to his son, who was in hospital.

After that it was just a succession of traitors, grasses and liars. I had studied the jury and I knew there was no chance we would get a result. They had been hand-picked. And not by us.

Finally, after thirty-eight days, the twelve members of the jury retired to consider their verdict. We went down to the cells to wait. We had lived well during the trial, we had eaten and drunk well, and fresh clothing had been brought to us every day, but we knew that all that was going to change. We were tense, we weren't scared, we were just tense. After seven hours we were told they were ready.

We were brought up one by one for sentencing. I was the first. The judge, Melford Stevenson, was wearing scarlet robes, and he had a black cap on the bench alongside him – the same black cap, I thought, which would have once been used to sentence men to death. He looked at me and said: 'I am not going to waste words on you. In my view society has earned a rest from your activities.' He repeated the charges against me. And the verdicts. Guilty, of course. Then he sentenced me to be detained at Her Majesty's pleasure for 'a minimum of thirty years'. It took sixteen minutes. In the time it would take to drink a nice glass of gin and tonic, he had thrown away the rest of my active life. It was gone. It was a fucking outrage.

Reg got thirty years minimum for the killing of McVitie;

Charlie got ten years for allegedly disposing of McVitie's body. The judge said to him: 'It may well be that you are not an active member of the Firm, but I am satisfied that you were an active helper in the dreadful enterprise of concealing the traces of the murder that your brothers committed.'

Tony and Chris Lambrianou got fifteen years; Ron Bender got twenty years; Connie Whitehead got seven years. Freddie Foreman, who was never a member of our Firm, got ten years for being an accessory to the McVitie killing; and Albert Donaghue got two years. Donaghue got away lightly after pleading guilty to being an accessory but, then, he had given the police a lot of help.

On Tuesday, 4 March, the thirty-ninth day of the trial, Anthony Barry was acquitted and discharged. Nipper Read's other informers, including Ronnie Hart, got away without being charged. Melford Stevenson then said: 'The debt the public owes to Superintendent Read and his officers cannot be overstated, and can never be discharged.'

Sadly for Nipper, not all of his colleagues felt the same way. In his autobiography he wrote:

> As the success of the operation became more apparent, feeling on the fifth floor changed to positive resentment that it was unable to share the story. This was not unusual. The same thing had happened in the Richardson case when every effort had been made to steer the limelight away from Gerry McArthur, the real author of its success. It was apparent that success in a major investigation such as his and mine is not the best way to further a career. As I learned, it can be distinctly detrimental.

Nipper should have thought about that before he started. But it still wasn't over for us. Three of us, me, Reg, and Freddie Foreman, had to face a new trial in the case of Frank Mitchell. We had a new judge, Mr Justice Lawton, and a new jury. It was a pointless and costly exercise. At the end of it all, after another twenty days, I was found not guilty of the murder of Mitchell. Reg got five years, to run concurrently with his life sentence for murder for freeing Frank from Dartmoor, and another nine months, also to run concurrently, for harbouring him. Freddie Foreman, whom the prosecution claimed had actually shot Frank Mitchell dead, was found not guilty. And rightly so.

By 25 May it was all over. It had taken two trials lasting sixty-three days, plus the huge costs of the investigation, the protection of the witnesses and the jury, hundreds of policemen and some of the best legal brains in the country just to put a handful of villains behind bars. Two of them, me and Reg, for at least thirty years. And others, like Ian Barrie – who had never killed anyone – for the best part of their active lives. What Melford Stevenson did was inhuman. And I am not the only person to think so. Shortly after the trial, Professor Leon Radzinwicz, Britain's leading authority at that time on long-term prison sentences, wrote in the *Sunday Times*: 'Society owes long-term prisoners something more than death in small doses.'

And Lord Soper, the Methodist leader, said: 'Thirty years is more horrible than hanging. The procedure of putting the Krays away and allowing them to rot is a more horrible fate than the quickness of a rope.' He added: 'Long-term prison sentences are an admission of failure. There has to be a ray of hope left for every man, whatever he has done.'

Una Padel, of the Prison Reform Trust, said: 'It was the high emotion surrounding the Kray case that led to such a harsh sentence.'

On Wednesday, 28 May, three days after the end of the trial, they began to disperse us. They sent us to prisons around the country because Read thought it was 'vital for security reasons' that we were split up. Me and Charlie went to Durham, but were separated the moment we got there, Reg went to Parkhurst, Freddie Foreman went to Leicester, Connie White-head went to Hull, and so on.

There were appeals on behalf of all defendants. They were heard in the High Court in the Strand in July 1969, but they got nowhere. The real battle for us was now just beginning. The battle to survive in the prison system. The police were happy, they had finally put away the Kray twins. As Nipper Read said, the moment the verdicts were announced at the original trial: 'I didn't look up . . . I was afraid that people would see the tears in my eyes.'

But was it just Read and the police who brought us down? Not according to a book called *The Evil Firm: The Rise and Fall of the Brothers Kray*, which was published shortly after the end of the trial. It was written by three *Daily Mirror* journalists, Brian McConnell, Tom Tullett and Edward Vale. This was not a pro-Kray book, it was very anti us. But the book shows that me and Reg were sunk not just by the traitors in our own Firm, but also by the Inland Revenue, who had been called in by someone close to the top of the Labour government of the day. That someone was probably the Home Secretary, James Callaghan, who was later to become prime minister. Questions had been asked about us in the House of Common, and the government were sensitive about suggestions that the police could not control us.

Brian McConnell, who was tracking our activities for the *Daily Mirror*, claims he was summoned to a secret government office in Shepherd's Bush, five miles from the centre of London, and told by a Special Inspector of the Inland Revenue that he must reveal all he knew about us – or else. And that his conversation with the agent was covered under the Offical Secrets Act.

McConnell wrote in his book: 'The Krays toiled at various activities but they did not spin their coins to the satisfaction of HM Government. It did not need a crystal ball to see they were under some sort of surveillance.' He also spoke of the 'many kinds of investigators engaged on the matters Kray'.

I believe there is clear evidence that there was a massive conspiracy, over many years, and involving many government departments, which had the sole aim of bringing us down. At our trial there were accusations in the press of government and police persecution and corruption. One newspaper spoke of 'an arch conspirator, a gross perverter of justice with a criminal soul, standing in such a strong position that even the courts are putty in his hands'.

I believe, at the end of the day, the government of England were even more corrupt and evil than they said we were.

CHAPTER FIVE

The Funny Farm

'The basic secrecy concerning Broadmoor reinforces the
public's fear and ignorance of the place. The public
probably has more knowledge of what is on Mars than they
have of what Broadmoor is like.'

Department of Health Internal Study

The patients call Broadmoor the 'funny farm' because of the
weird things that happen here. Sometimes they are amusing,
sometimes they are sad. Often they are quite moving. I'll give
you an example. One day I was sitting in a hut in the kitchen
gardens with a group of patients. Since I met my wife, Kate, I've
got interested in gardening. I like working on the plants and
vegetables and watching them grow, it relaxes me. Anyway, we
were just having a short break from our work, a cup of tea and a
smoke. Suddenly, an old man called Chris got on his knees on
the stone floor and started to pray. He's not a religious man, just
a sinner and a patient like the rest of us. But he was oblivious to

everyone and everything, and it was the most spontaneous act of prayer I've ever seen in my life.

That's the sort of thing you could only see in the funny farm. In the middle of all the hate and sadness, a moment of genuine emotion. You get it all here, you see every kind of man here, every kind of problem. And I've seen it all because I've been here a long time. They sent me here on 25 July 1979. I cannot forget that date because after the hell I went through at Parkhurst prison I was pleased to get here. It was a good day for me.

It was Nobby Clark who told me that Broadmoor can be heaven or hell, it just depends on you. He told me that in Parkhurst too: he said that if you behave yourself it's heaven, but if you misbehave they'll make your life hell. And it's true. Nobby had a troubled life and he was sent crazy by those bastards at Parkhurst. Finally, he couldn't take any more. He speared a coloured feller, stabbed him when he was lying in the bath. Did him up good and proper. So they sent him here.

Nobby had long grey hair and a long grey beard and bright twinkling eyes. He eventually died here after a heart attack. But I'll never forget what he told me about Broadmoor. Because he got it right. Dead right.

I've nearly always chosen to play by the rules at Broadmoor and, if it hasn't always been heaven, well, it hasn't been hell either. Nowhere near as bad as it would have been if I'd stayed at Parkhurst. That place was a nightmare. When Melford Stevenson sent us down in 1969 I was sent to Durham prison, in the north-east of England. My older brother, Charlie, was sent to the same prison, and so was Ian Barrie, who had been a loyal member of the Firm. We were all kept well apart, though, segregated from the moment we arrived at the jail. Reggie was sent to Parkhurst.

Durham prison is a bastard place and some right bastards worked there. From the word go, certain of the screws [warders] made it very clear they were going to kick the shit out of me every chance they got. Never one on one, of course, no, just a gang of them against me. They saw me as a hard man who had to be broken, not a feller who could be sick in the head with depression, who needed treatment. They had a simple technique and you can see it in any prison anywhere in the world. They torment, harass and wind up a con until he can take no more and retaliates. That then gives them the chance to give the con a good hiding. The punches and kicks and beatings from their clubs are always aimed at the body, never at the face. That way the beating doesn't show. Then the con is given days or weeks, sometimes months, in the punishment block. Locked up for twenty-three hours a day, every day, in solitary confinement, with no one and nothing for company. If you're lucky you get an hour's exercise walking by yourself in a tiny yard. You're always watched, of course, day and night. And there's always an electric light burning in your cell. You sleep, because you are bored and depressed; there's nothing else to do except sleep and think. But they'll always wake you up, just for the hell of it, and they'll always try to wind you up, gee you up, whenever they can. It passes the time for the screws.

Eventually, they throw you back into the main prison system and it all starts up again. It's all done for a purpose, of course. It's designed to break a con's body and his spirit, and it's very effective. Ask the Gestapo and the KGB, they had it down to a fine art. Only the strong survive and, funnily enough, some cons become even stronger because of it. But if you have a physical or mental problem to begin with, you have no chance. I do not say that every screw in every jail in Britain is like this, but I can say that in the three years I was in Durham prison I can only remember one screw with any humanity in him.

That was a senior officer called Chief Bunker. On one occasion, when four or five screws were giving me a good kicking while I lay on the floor trying to curl up and protect my head, I heard him shout out: 'That's enough, stop beating him.' I've never forgotten that one single act of decency and even now I still send him a Christmas card every year.

I realize, looking back, that my reputation and the publicity surrounding our case meant that I was bound to be the one the screws were looking for. Make no mistake, I'm not whining. I could take and dish out punishment as much as any other con, and more than most when I was young and fit, but the treatment I was getting was over the top. Our mother could see what had been happening every time she came to visit me at Durham, she could see the cuts and bruises from the beatings, and she could see that mentally I was going to pieces. So she started a campaign to get me moved away from Durham to Parkhurst, where she thought I would get better treatment and where I would also be close to Reggie. She sent a lot of letters to the Home Office, to our MP and to the press.

In 1972 I was finally moved to Parkhurst prison, on the Isle of Wight. I know the island itself is an attractive little place, but the prison is an old and dismal place. Reg hadn't got on too bad there, but I had a lot of problems right from the start. The screws were nearly as bad as the ones at Durham, and there was also aggravation from some of the other cons. Reg had warned me the screws would try to wind me up. When he first got there one of the screws said to another screw: 'Did Richardson get his visiting form?' The other one turned to see if Reg was watching, and said: 'You mean Eddie? Yes, he did.' This was a deliberate reference to Eddie Richardson, who was also at Parkhurst. Eddie and his brother Charlie had been the leaders of the gang who were our biggest rivals in London and there had been a lot of talk in the gutter press that the Richardsons were still out to get the Krays, even though we were all behind bars. It wasn't true, but the screws just wanted to get Reggie wound up, get him agitated, make him more likely to say or do the wrong thing. Then, wallop, in they would go and give him a good hiding. It would have suited them, anyway, to get things stirred up between

Reg and Eddie, get them at each other's throat. But Reg was too smart to fall for that one. He knew what they were trying to do and he didn't bite.

With me, though, it was easier. Because of my mental problems I had always gone off quicker than Reg if anyone upset me or slighted me. The screws knew that and used it. Also, in a big nick like Parkhurst you always have to watch your back, because there's always other cons who may carry a grudge from something which happened years ago, or young cons who want to make a name for themselves by getting a 'name' con like a Kray. That's one of the reasons Reg has kept himself so fit and hard over the years; he's had to. And even now he's getting on a bit it would take a brave con, or a stupid one, to try it on with my brother.

But things really started to go wrong for me at Parkhurst because of an assistant governor. I was very friendly with a particular con, who was a smashing feller. One day he was very upset because his mother had died of cancer. Like a lot of us, he had been very close to his mother and the news had gutted him. I wanted to show my respect to my friend's mother, so I put in an application to send a wreath to her funeral. When you are a Category A con you have to put in an application for just about everything. You almost have to put in an application to go and have a shit. But I didn't expect to have any problems over sending some flowers to a funeral.

However, this governor called me to his office and I could tell from the mean look on his face that this wasn't going to be straightforward, at all. He said to me: 'Kray, who are these flowers for?'

I told him they were for my friend's mother and I wanted his permission to get them sent.

'Well, Kray,' the bastard sneered, 'permission is refused.'

Just like that. And that, as far as he was concerned, was the end of the matter. I could've smashed him to a pulp, but I didn't. All I did was swear at him and that cost me another seven days in chokey [solitary confinement]. Another week locked up by myself, twenty-three hours a day, basic rations. After that it was downhill all the way, more trouble, more fights.

In my time at Parkhurst they did me for about twenty assaults and one charge of GBH. But that was only what they did me for. In the seven years I was in Parkhurst I got involved in a lot more scraps than that. I also smashed up my cell a few times in frustration. Really did it over. I couldn't help myself.

When I was in solitary confinement, which was a lot, they used to lock me in what they called the Strongbox. And that's just what it was, really. It was a room, but it was built in the shape of a small box. It was really dark and claustrophobic. The whole room was made of concrete, including a little bed in the middle. They used to give me one blanket. Sometimes I didn't even get that. I used to have to sleep on the slab of cold stone that was the bed. It was not a nice place. There was a tiny exercise yard well away from the other prisoners, to keep me separate.

The screws were bastards. Cruel bastards. There was one kind man, a medical officer called David Cooper. He let me take a radio to the Strongbox, to give me a bit of company. Funnily enough, at the end of my time in Parkhurst, it was on that radio that I heard I was being moved to Broadmoor. They announced it on the BBC radio news – and I was listening to it in the Strongbox.

But all that was a long time after my row with the assistant governor over sending flowers to the funeral of Pete Gattrell's mother. That was really the turning point for me. That was when I really started to go downhill. Fast. I sank into a hell of a depression, the worst I've ever known. All I could see was years and years in front of me as a Category A con with constant supervision, restricted visits, no perks, and constant harassment. It was just a hopeless existence. My paranoia was getting worse all the time; my head hurt me, the pain was bad. I could feel the walls closing in on me, I could feel trouble all around me, I felt round every corner someone was waiting to jump me. I had some more fights with screws, more chokey, and then I had a real bad fight with another con. I can't remember what it was about, but I think I hurt him bad. After that they gave up on me. The medical officer at Parkhurst said I was insane, said I was a menace and they were going to get rid of me. On 25 July 1979, they did. They sent me to Broadmoor. And do you know something? When they told me I was coming here, when they told me they were going to send me to a lunatic asylum, I was pleased. For me it meant seven years of hell at Parkhurst were over. You see, I knew what they didn't know, what they never bothered to try and find out, because they didn't really care. I knew I was sick, really sick. When I came to Broadmoor the doctors here explained to me, for the first time in my life, that I am a chronic paranoid schizophrenic. That doesn't mean I'm a raving lunatic, because I'm not. But it does mean I am ill and need medical help. Since then I've done a lot of reading up on illness of the mind. The doctors here encourage you to learn about your illness, to try and understand it. That way you have more of a chance of beating it, or at least coming to terms with it, living with it.

The difference is that Broadmoor is a hospital, it is not a prison. It is a hospital for the criminally insane. It comes under the Health department, not the Home Office, though the Home Office has to grant permission for a patient's release. The staff here are not warders, they are nurses. Because it is a hospital, someone like me has a much better chance of the right care and attention. In prison, someone like me is just regarded as a headbanger, a trouble-maker.

This kind of approach to mental illness is fairly new and it doesn't work with all patients, but it has helped me. My own reading has told me that schizophrenia means I have a split personality, a mind that can work in two ways virtually at the same time. Schizophrenia causes severe depression and that creates other problems. In my case when I'm going into a depression, going into one, as I call it, one part of my mind creates suspicion, really bad suspicion that becomes paranoia. If I see two people talking together, my mind tells me they could be talking about me, could be plotting about me. Then my brain will tell me to go and stop them. It doesn't matter how, but they must be stopped. It's something, I now realize, that I have suffered from for many, many years, maybe for most of my life. It sounds simple, but it isn't. The most difficult thing about mental illness is trying to work out in your mind what is normal and what isn't normal, what is right and what isn't right. Believe me, insanity is a terrible sensation. They have shown me at Broadmoor how to recognize when I am going into one, how to read the signs, how to control the paranoia I feel by taking drugs. I now know what medication to take and when to take it. With the help of my drugs I have learned how to control my madness, if that's what you want to call it.

My schizophrenia would have started very early in my life, as it does with most people. And the simple fact is, it was something beyond my control. There was nothing I could have done about it. Most schizophrenics have ancestors or relations with mental disorders. In my own case, my own mental problems may be traced back to my great grandfather, Critcha Lee, who was a gypsy and a cattle dealer from Bermondsey and died in Claybury madhouse. My grandfather's brother, who they called Jewy, also died there. I have traced back our family roots a long way and my earliest ancestors probably came from Austria – even today, the surname Kray is quite common in the Salzburg area. But it does seem that the family have had a lot of mental problems over the years, although both my parents were very sane and normal people.

But what causes schizophrenia? I have read up on it and a child can be a schizophrenic even before it is born. Something goes wrong in the chemistry of a baby's body, even when it is still inside its mother, but the problems don't show up until a lot later. You can tell kids who may be schizophrenic – kids who are backward, or precocious, or day-dreamers, or kids who fly into tempers. I wasn't backward but I suppose I always had a bit of a temper on me. I still do, but I can usually control it with will-power and drugs.

I know about my drugs and I know about the ways in which they help me. I take Stemetol capsules four times a day to quieten my nerves. I also take Disipal which is for the side-effects caused by the Stemetol, which sometimes makes my limbs shake and difficult to control. Every fortnight I have an injection of Modicate, which is a drug specifically to curb the symptoms of schizophrenia. It stops the bad dreams and the depressions.

What none of them can cure – what nothing can cure – when I'm going into one is the terrible feeling of loneliness. You see, drugs can only do so much. The most important thing for a mentally ill person is their peace of mind. Some of the poor people who suffer from mental illness never have peace of mind. They suffer in their minds all their lives, they are tormented souls. There are some terrible cases here at Broadmoor, men and women who are so badly disturbed in their minds that they never recover. These people deserve pity and understanding, not condemnation. That's why patients in Broadmoor rarely gang up on other patients. Why even men like Peter Sutcliffe, the Yorkshire Ripper, are relatively safe here, which they wouldn't be in a prison. Because the patients here know that other patients cannot help the things they have done.

Some people do get better, some regain such control over their own minds that they are released. I like to think I am among those winning the battle against this illness, but it's a long and lonely road. Patients can see for themselves how well, or how badly, they are doing. Every few years each one goes before a mental health tribunal which decides how well he or she is progressing, and whether the patient is in a state of mind where freedom or a change of hospital would be suitable. That hasn't happened to me yet. But I know that things are getting better. I'll tell you why. When I had a review in June 1983, it wasn't good. Dr D. Tidmarsh, who was my consultant psychiatrist, wrote this:

> Ronald Kray is a chronic schizophrenic. In what for him is the unstressful environment of Broadmoor his illness does not become florid and its symptoms are, more or less, controlled by medication. I am sure, however, that he would relapse if he were under stress, as he would be if he were returned to prison. As he is the first to admit, he can no longer stand the pace of prison or, I believe, the competition from younger prisoners and, in that environment, I am sure he would decompensate rapidly with the risk of further violence.

Like I say, not a great report. But when I went before the review tribunal in 1991, this is what they said:

> Dr Ferris reported well upon this patient and it is clear that his psychotic condition is now well controlled by medication and by the patient's own insight into any early onset of his illness.

I still didn't get freedom, of course, or even a move to a softer hospital, but that, to me, was a good report and proof to me that I do understand my own mind better than I ever did.

All the patients here get visits and checks from social workers and they put in their own reports on us. I have managed to get hold of a recent report on me by a senior social worker called Mrs Carol Parkinson. She said about me:

> Mr Kray's wife, Kate, visits her husband on a regular basis and offers him support. Mr Kray also has a considerable number of friends who write and visit. Mr Kray has recently transferred to a new ward in the hospital where he seems to have settled in well. He works four mornings

each week in the kitchen gardens and spends the rest of his time listening to music or reading on the wards. When eventually discharged, Mr Kray hopes to live with his wife in a house in the country. He presently requires regular medication to control the symptoms of mental illness and it would therefore seem in his best clinical interest to remain in Broadmoor for the foreseeable future.

So I know, from that, that I am still going to be here for some time, maybe for ever. That doesn't worry me. But I would like to get out one day, go and live in the country and travel to places like India and Africa. I have had a premonition that I won't ever be set free, a very real premonition. But, on the other hand, one of the doctors here told a friend of mine that I could be set free one day. I just don't know.

I will never forget the day I came to Broadmoor, because no patient ever does. It was a lovely sunny day in 1979, and I thought the sunshine was a good omen. I couldn't wait to get here. When they threw me out of Parkhurst it was one of the happiest days of my life. They brought me here in a van with five screws. I remember we came over on the ferry from Ryde to Portsmouth – me stuck in the prison van all the way, of course – and when we got to Portsmouth there was a screw from Parkhurst on the harbourside waiting to travel back to the Isle of Wight.

The driver of the prison van stopped to talk to this screw and I heard the screw say: 'Who've you got in there, then? Another fucking geriatric?' They all had a good laugh about that, but I thought it was me who was having the last laugh. I was getting away from Parkhurst, they were stuck with the God-forsaken place. I remember arriving here. I can remember the van driving off the main road into what seemed to be a big park. Then, through the tiny window in the side of the van, I saw a big sign on a white board: 'Broadmoor Special Hospital. Private Property'.

We drove up a hill which seemed to get steeper and steeper.

There were some beautiful tall trees. Pine trees. Right at the top of the hill it seemed to get dark, like the trees were closing in, and then I saw the hospital for the first time. It was big. Big and silent. Depressing, really. All dark red bricks and high walls. Nowadays, they tell me, the hospital has a smart entrance hall, but when I came here none of that existed. We drove through two huge wooden doors and then through some giant padlocked gates into the main courtyard. It was real quiet, a bit spooky, and there seemed to be no one around. Just big blocks, the hospital wards, all around the courtyard. I was taken to what they call the admission ward and met by some nurses and a social worker. I was weighed and my height was measured and then I was told to get into a bath. The male nurses, the screws, stood watching me all the time. The heavy atmosphere, the staff presence, is deliberate: it's designed to have a psychological effect of intimidation on potentially troublesome patients. It works.

After my bath I was given a cup of tea, and locked up in a bare room about nine feet long and six feet wide, with just a mattress on the floor and some bedding. There was a big, wooden shutter across the window, so there was no light. Only the electric light bulb which was never turned off. Next to the door was a slit through which the staff could stand and watch you. An hour before the night staff came on duty I was unlocked and given a cigarette, and they told me what would happen to me over the next few weeks. They told me that the first few days and weeks at Broadmoor are the most difficult for every patient – but how he reacted to them would affect his whole future in the hospital. I remembered Nobby Clark's words: If you behave yourself, it's heaven. If you don't behave yourself . . .

The admission floor was on the bottom of Somerset House, where I eventually finished up living for many years. Everyone has to come through the admission ward. The daily routine here was weird and hard to get used to. In the morning we were unlocked at seven o'clock. We slopped out – got rid of our own urine and excrement, our own mess from the night before – then had a wash and a shave, and had to line up while we waited for the razors to be counted. They weren't taking any chances because a lot of patients have suicidal tendencies.

When this was over, I and the other new arrivals went into the day room, where we just sat all day until nine o'clock at night. Again, the system is designed to put you under psychological pressure, so the staff can assess how you react. Make a wrong move and life would be harder in the future. The rooms, like all the buildings here in those days, were drab and depressing. Relics from another age. They should all have been condemned years ago. They were all like poorhouses. To use the toilet you had to be escorted there and back by a screw, who stood and waited for you outside the cubicle and stuck his head over the top if he thought you were taking too long. If you had a bath you were given six inches of water in case you tried to drown yourself and the screws, the nurses, were watching all the time. It was humiliating.

In the day room, there were five rows of chairs across the room, and a television set at the end. Down the side of the room was a line of blue chairs where the staff sat and watched our every move. They were there, as well, to listen to our conversation. But no one said much, so that was a waste of time. Also in the day room was a small table and chair where you could write letters, and a small snooker table. That's all. That was to be my life for the next three months.

Just off the day room was the dining hall, and the thing that surprised me was, the food was not bad. Plain, simple food, like that in hospital, but not bad. And we had china cups and proper knives and forks. The food was better than in prison, where we never had proper knives and forks, either, just plastic ones. Breakfast was at eight, lunch at twelve, tea at five. After every meal all the knives and forks were counted. For obvious reasons, before we were moved back into the day room.

A few weeks on, after washing and breakfast I was given a

few odd jobs to do, and I just dragged the jobs out as long as I could, made them last as long as possible, to cut down the boredom of the endless days doing nothing.

During those early weeks and months you are seen by an endless stream of doctors, psychologists, education officers and social workers – and assessed by them all. The simple, basic rules of the hospital are explained to you. Behave yourself, and you will get privileges: a better room in a softer block, the freedom to work where you want, the use of a radio. Misbehave, and you are in bother. Serious bother. You will be put in solitary confinement. In Norfolk House, the punishment block. Word had gone round about Norfolk House, the 'House of Correction' as some members of the staff cynically call it. The hospital prefers to call it the intensive care unit. Call it what you want, it's a bad place to be. It is still the most feared part of the hospital. It looks and is a frightening place. There are rumours about Norfolk House, but I have no proof of anyone being physically abused in there, or being abused with drugs, as others have claimed. But the psychological pressure and intimidation inside that building has to be experienced to be realized. I believe that you could go in there sane and come out mad. The rules are simple – attack another patient and you will get at least forty-eight hours in solitary; attack a nurse and you will get at least a week. In the old days patients could spend weeks, months, even years in Norfolk House. Some, it's said, never came out again.

Only once, in the early days, did I step out of line, and they put me into Norfolk House for five months. I started getting into fights with screws. I was silly. After that I chose a more sensible path and I have not been back since. Norfolk House is ugly. From behind its barred windows you can hear the cries of the patients. Cries of anguish. The torment of pain. Not physical pain but something far worse – mental agony.

I got through my first three months on the admission ward and was then taken to Somerset House, or Block C as it was called in those days. This was a total contrast to what I had just experienced. Somerset House had its own rules, ward policies and regulations, of course, but it was known as one of the friendlier houses in the hospital and I soon settled into it. My new life had begun and I began to adapt to it.

CHAPTER SIX

This Is My Life

'Half the population of Broadmoor could be discharged –
the problem is knowing which half.'

                                    Former Broadmoor Medical Officer

The story of Broadmoor is as complex and controversial as
the place itself. Only when you study its past do you realize
why it is the way it is today. Did you know, for example, that
Broadmoor was originally built because of a madman with a gun
and a king of England who later became mad? As Michael Caine
might say, not many people know that!

I know as much as anyone about this place. But then, I
suppose, I ought to! I started to learn about the hospital from a
book in the library here. It is called *Broadmoor: A History of
Criminal Lunacy and Its Problems*, and it was written in the early
1950s by a man called Ralph Partridge. A lot of the book has
become out of date in the past forty years, of course, and
Partridge sounds like a bit of a goody-goody, trying to paint the
sort of picture of Broadmoor that he knew the authorities would

like. But it was a starting point, with government and health service documents (some of which I shouldn't have seen), newspapers, photographs and conversations with older patients and staff at the hospital, in my search for the real Broadmoor.

One thing you have to come to terms with very early here is this: you no longer have any rights or powers. You are a surname and a number. You live by rules and regulations – other people's. And you have to get along with the patients around you. All of them. Even those you hate.

Normally, in prison, grasses, ponces, sex offenders and people like that are avoided. If they cause any problems at all they are beaten or cut. Here in Broadmoor it doesn't happen like that. You have to accept that, no matter how bad a person may be, and no matter how horrendous the crime they have committed, if they are here it is because they suffer from some sort of psychological disorder. In other words, what they have done is beyond their control. I don't like mixing with such people but I have to put up with it. I try and avoid them. I have never liked sex offenders or men who have hurt old people or children. So I let it be known that these men should stay away from me. They get the message.

Everyone here thinks about freedom, though it doesn't worry me too much. But I still go through the same process as everyone else. Every year you are entitled to a tribunal, every three years you have a compulsory tribunal. The process is very simple. You get your own medical officer's report, your own independent doctor's report and your social worker's report. You can be represented by a solicitor, but I don't bother. I know they won't let me out. Not yet.

The tribunal is made up of a judge, a doctor and what they call a lay person, a member of the public. But you learn early on in your time here that very few people are discharged by a tribunal. The only real way out for a Section 65 patient, a convicted murderer, is if your psychiatrist here is convinced you

ve Left: Me and my Alsatian, Freda. We used to spend hours wandering across bomb sites in London. Our parents always encouraged us to be kind to animals.

ve Right: A proud moment. This is me aged twelve receiving the Keymer Cup off the Mayor of Bethnal Green for winning a Hackney boxing championship.

Below: Reg and me at our first fight at the Mile End Arena.

Above: Young actor – I appeared as an extra (*far right*) in *The Magic Box* starring Robert Donat.

Right: Mum with Sonny Liston, once the heavyweight boxing champion of the world.

Below: This is me with my mum and Grandmother Lee.

Above: A cocktail with my friends Lord Boothby and Leslie Holt.

low: Lord Effingham and me down the Kentucky Club, in 1963. Effingham stood as our front man in the first of our ventures in the West End.

Above: Down to business with 'Mr Fixit', Joe Kaufman, who was to be our contact and middle man with the Mafia.

OSITE PAGE

o Left: Me and Reg. We always liked to k smart to do business.

o Right: Here I am with Dot. She the gypsy's curse on Judge Melford venson – it cost him his sight.

ove Left: George Cornell. No one liked . He was a flash, arrogant bully. He d McVitie cost us half our lives. It is ause of them that we were put away. *ndication International*)

ove Right: Jack 'The Hat' McVitie. He d to wear a hat to hide his bald head. *ndication International*)

ht: Charlie Richardson. We had a kind rrangement that his gang controlled the derworld south of the river while me and g took control of the East. *ess Association*)

Above Left: Outside the Blind Begga[r]
the night I shot Cornell.
(*Press Association*)

Left: Leonard 'Nipper' Read. 'Nippe[r]
takes the credit for doing me and R[eg]
(*Press Association*)

Above Right: My brother, Charlie,
outside the mansion he, me and Reg
bought in Suffolk. Maybe one day w[e]
can all be there together.

Right: Lennie Peters and Di Lee of
Peters and Lee. It was because of us
that Lennie got his first singing brea[k]

Above Left: My beautiful new wife Kate with Roy Shaw, a long-time friend of mine, at our wedding reception. I was not allowed out for

Left: My trusted friend Wilf Pine.

Above Right: My favourite picture o Kate, taken by Lord Lichfield. I kee next to my bed so I can see it when go to bed at night and wake up in t morning.

are fit to be discharged, and if he can then persuade the Home Secretary. Only then will a patient like me be released.

You think about it a lot when you first come here. But as the months and the years go by, you come to terms with it all. And, if you've got any sense, you just get on with it and make the most of your life at the Funny Farm. Life here has got a lot better for me and the other patients who have been moved into new blocks. For many years my home was Somerset House, one of the oldest buildings here. It was a tiny room with bars on the window, bleak and depressing. It was small and claustrophobic. Dark and cold. The only nice thing about it was the view through the narrow window. I could see trees and fields. The room was kept locked. Along the corridor were the wash basins and toilets which we all shared. The majority of patients in Broadmoor still live like that. It's like something out of another age.

I get angry when I read how some of the newspapers have described my life. For example, the *Star* wrote in June 1983: 'Ronnie Kray will have smoked salmon for his supper tonight, with thinly sliced brown bread and Normandy butter – all delivered specially from Harrods, the top people's store.' Stories like this are lies. So are stories that I 'rule' Broadmoor, that I live in luxury here, even stories that rent boys have been shipped into the hospital to keep me company in a private room. Complete lies. The trouble is, some people believe them, including some Members of Parliament who ought to know better. I am treated no differently from any other patient here. My life is as harsh as theirs.

In 1993 the *Star* ran a story that Peter Sutcliffe, the Yorkshire Ripper, was upset because I have more visitors than him and that my visitors do not have to be vetted. Again, lies. I have the same number of visitors as every other patient and, just like them, all my visitors have to go through a security check before they are allowed to come and see me. Some are refused. These newspaper stories cause me problems here. I have *never*

83

been treated any differently from anyone else. It took years, for example, before I was allowed to have a small record player in my room. I argued my case with the chief medical officer here at the time. I asked him what the difference was between music played on a record player and music played on the radio. I told him, 'You should let me have a record player, you should let all patients who want one. It will make your job easier, because music soothes a troubled mind.' Eventually he relented and he let me have one on trial, so long as I didn't play it too loud. The experiment worked and I was the first patient allowed to keep a record player. Now lots of patients have them, and far more sophisticated machinery, too.

But it was a real battle to win one small privilege. There is little luxury for the patient here. One of our real perks is the hospital shop where each patient is allowed to have an account which we have to pay off monthly. No one is allowed to handle real money. Patients use social security money, plus hospital wages and gifts from family and friends to buy sweets, toothpaste, soap, tea, coffee, cigarettes, newspapers and magazines. All the newspapers are censored by the hospital and any article which could upset patients is cut out. We still see them eventually, of course. I use a lot of my money to buy writing paper, envelopes and stamps. I get hundreds of letters and I try to reply to some of them. But I wish people didn't write to me. I am grateful for their support and their messages, but it's too much for me to try and reply to them all.

For many years after I came here I didn't do any work at all, apart from cleaning my own room. Now I work in the kitchen gardens four mornings a week growing vegetables and flowers. It passes the time and I enjoy it. Boredom is the biggest enemy here. There is just so much time to kill. An official Government Study Project a few years ago highlighted the monotony of everyday life in Broadmoor. The project's account of an average day in the life of a patient is still relevant today. It makes for gloomy reading. It says:

THIS IS MY LIFE

6.55 a.m.   The staff unlock the patients' siderooms
                     and/or dormitories.

6.55–7.20 a.m.   The patients wash and dress and make their
                     beds.

7.20–8.00 a.m.   Patients go to day room and have a cup of
                     tea.

8.00 a.m.   Assemble in the dining room for breakfast.

8.30 a.m.   Return to day room. Receive medication
                     and make any preparation (if any) to go to
                     the occupation room.

9.00–11.45 a.m.   Patients go to the occupation areas
                     (weekdays only) escorted by nursing staff.
                     When there, they receive instruction from
                     the occupation officers. Some mornings they
                     may go to the school, dentist, optician,
                     group therapy or the shop.

11.45 a.m.   Return to wards, wash and assemble for
                     lunch.

12 noon   Lunch, as for breakfast.

12.30 p.m.   Return under escort to the ward, have
                     medication, use the day and rest rooms for
                     recreation; such things as having a cup of
                     tea, chatting to friends, listening to the
                     radio or watching television, or reading
                     library or private books, or writing letters.
                     The choice of activity at this time rests
                     solely with the patient since this hour is an
                     official break from required activities.

1.30 p.m.	Assemble and return to occupation area, the procedure to be followed (as mentioned above at 9.00 a.m.) until 3.40, when the patients stop work and wait for the checking of tools and materials in the occupation area, by the occupation officers.
3.45 p.m.	Return from work departments.
4.00 p.m.	Tea, as for breakfast. Patients counted.
4.30 p.m.	Return to ward, have medication. Bathrooms, siderooms, dormitories, washrooms and tearoom doors are opened by staff. The patients may have a bath and may use the rest room or recreation area of their choice on the ward, or they may wish to do their domestic work, such as washing their clothes or other private linen. Washing machine, tumble dryer and drying room are provided in some wards.
6.30 p.m.	Assemble for a visit to the house garden or airing courts for fresh air and sunshine. Proceed, under nursing staff escort, to the garden where they may indulge in tennis, badminton, football practice, gardening, or they may wish to have a purposeful walk with one or more of their friends and fellow patients, or they might just wish to sit or lie in the garden and relax.
7.20 p.m.	Return to the ward and answer the day roll-call.
7.30 p.m.	Have supper on the ward, served by nursing staff. Continue indoor recreational activities or personal domestic chores. This, patients

may do with or without staff participation, although staff observation is maintained throughout the day. Available to the patient at this time are: card playing, record playing, cassette tape replay, table tennis, snooker, watching TV or listening to the radio. All activities are observed by staff and supervised where necessary, so that individual patients may derive maximum benefit when they participate.

8.30 p.m.   Change from house clothes to bed clothes and dressing gowns.

8.45 p.m.   Report to the clinical room for night sedation.

9.00 p.m.   Go to bed and be locked in rooms.

The Study Project concludes: 'Some telling facts emerge from this official "average" schedule. Apart from medication and the periods devoted to occupational therapy, the bulk of the day is not spent in any kind of therapeutic activity. It is left to the environment to improve the patient.' The authorities would probably say that this report is now out of date and that things have improved in the 'new' Broadmoor. Well, so they have. But the patients here will still tell you that there is an awful lot of time left to kill, especially for those who can't or won't work.

The general manager, Alan Franey, has done his best to improve the facilities and conditions, and he has succeeded, but there is still not enough equipment or staff – and there never will be, because there's never enough money. It's like the buildings here. The new buildings are good, but the old buildings still stand because, again, the money has run out. A lot of patients still live in the old part of the hospital. It's a depressing place. Because the institution is built in such drab colours, dark red bricks and grey roof slates, when it's raining its gloomy colours reflect the mood of the weather, and the mood of those locked up. Even the birds seem to be institutionalized. You don't see them until mealtimes when suddenly hundreds appear, and all of them tame and friendly. Like us, it seems, they live by the clock.

The birds are lucky. When they get tired of this place they can simply move on. For the patients it's not that easy, although one or two have managed to get away – even in these days when security is very tight – and even though the authorities had started to boast, foolishly, that Broadmoor was 'escape-proof'. In 1991, a patient called James Saunders escaped. Saunders, known as the Wolfman, was a child rapist, and he used a hacksaw blade to saw through the bars of a window. He never said if he got the blade from someone who came in to visit him, or if he stole it from builders who were working at the hospital at the time.

A year later, a nurse found a hacksaw blade among the belongings of Peter Sutcliffe, the Ripper. The authorities assumed that *had* been brought in and security checks on visitors were really stepped up. At one time visitors were bringing all sorts into the hospital, drugs, booze, everything, but they've really tightened up on that sort of thing. Nowadays all your visitors have to be strictly vetted before they are allowed to visit you. Security is paramount, it comes before everything else in the hospital. The staff have been doing it for so long that they have more or less perfected it.

There's an old saying in the hospital that if three patients were planning to escape, two of them would tell their favourite nurse about it! Observation by nursing staff is a key factor in the security, and the nurses know almost everything that goes on among the staff and the patients. Certain patients, of course, 'feed' the staff with information because they think it will make their own lives easier. Such patients are not encouraged. You could say they are discouraged. They are warned and perhaps pushed around a bit if they continue. Any patient who thinks he or she can get round the incredible security here is usually heavily mistaken. Some have discovered this to their cost. All movement throughout the hospital, by patients and staff, is closely watched, via television and video cameras, in the central control room. This is the heart of the hospital and the staff always know where every patient is, at any time of the day or night. If they want to check, they use the cameras to hunt out the patient, wherever he may be. Big Brother is always watching, whether you are waking, sleeping, or simply having a crap.

Some members of the nursing staff have walkie-talkie radios and it is their job to let the central control room know how many patients are leaving a given area, and where they are going to. At the other end of the transit another nurse with a radio lets control know that he has safely received the correct number of patients. It's a constant numbers game. If ever there is a miscount and the total doesn't tally, the control room instantly calls for a spot check. At that moment all movement within the hospital stops. And a total re-count of patients then takes place. Nothing and no one moves until everyone has been checked and rechecked. Only when control is satisfied that every patient has been accounted for, do things return to normal and the hospital continues its everyday routine.

The wall around Broadmoor is the highest I have ever seen. It is higher than the Berlin wall and has probably broken nearly as many hearts and minds. The wall has two psychological effects on the patients, most of whom – especially in the early days – think about escaping. Firstly, how do you scale such an enormous obstacle, thirty feet high at its lowest point? Secondly, the bigness, thickness and solidity of the wall is designed to make patients feel 'comfortable' and secure within it. It is like a big red blanket all around you. It smothers any desire to escape, except in the most determined of people. An infra-red beam goes around the wall as a further security measure. The beam is so sensitive it can be broken even by a small bird or bat flying through it. Nursing staff patrol the wall and if the infra-red beam is broken it immediately alerts control, and another spot check is called for. Once again the whole hospital grinds to a halt. It happens often. No patient ever does go over that wall, though. If and when anyone does get out, it's through the bars, and the spot check will quickly reveal who the missing person is. Then the staff have to carry out a complete search of the hospital and its grounds. Not easy, and it takes time because the hospital is big and there are many hiding places. The grounds are bigger still – 416 acres in all, including 53 acres within the security perimeter.

While the search is going on the police are alerted and a photograph of the missing patient is sent by fax to all the police stations in the area. Sirens are sounded to warn local people that a Broadmoor patient is on the run. Several of these sirens are scattered around the countryside within a 15-mile radius of Broadmoor. Police roadblocks are also set up. Like I say, it is not an easy place to escape from, though it has been done. Security on the wards is a big part of our everyday routine. During the day patients are counted when they are unlocked in the mornings and at every mealtime, after work periods and when they are locked up at night. We are also counted before and after visits. All wards have walkie-talkies for staff and alarm bells in case of a fight or a patient becoming disturbed. When the alarm bells go off on a ward, staff on that ward all move in to bring the trouble under control. And staff from other wards are on stand-by to help them if necessary. Help is not normally required. The staff tend to be big fellers, they are usually armed with clubs, and they are trained in the techniques of 'restraint'. They try not to hurt patients but, if a good kicking is the way to bring a situation under control, then so be it. Sometimes you will get a nurse who likes to hurt patients, who will use physical violence whenever possible, but then, to be fair, some of the patients like a scrap as well. It's all part of the tensions and frustrations you get in a place like this, particularly during a very hot summer when tempers easily boil over.

Fire is another risk, especially in a place full of arsonists! If the fire alarm goes off, all the staff and patients on the affected ward are counted up and then moved to a safe area. The fire brigade always sends round three fire engines within minutes. All the security and alarm systems are tested every week. Even when you are asleep you are checked by staff every fifteen minutes throughout the night. They look through the spyhole in your door or even open your room up, if they want to. It's all what *they* want. As I said, if you are a patient you have no rights.

But even the security here was put to the test during the massive changes in the autumn of 1990. That was when I, my friend Charlie Smith and other patients from Somerset House were moved into a brand-new block called Oxford House. Charlie and I were told we would be on Henley Ward, on the first floor. The move took four days. Everything had to be packed in boxes and then moved by lorry to the new building. But it was worth all the aggravation because the change it made to our living conditions was incredible. In Somerset House we all had to slop out every morning, we never had our own toilet. All the washing and toilet facilities were down the end of the corridor. Four sinks for thirty patients and not even the toilets had any privacy. Our rooms had no facilities at all. The place was always cold. Our new rooms have toilets and washbasins. There is no more slopping out, which I believe should be banned from every hospital and prison. It is a degrading thing, it takes away a man's dignity. The new rooms are like a large plastic mould, they are easy to clean and we even have a built-in wardrobe. In the old rooms you had to hang all your clothes on a hook on the door. You can have the curtains and bedcovers you want, as long as you pay for them, and ornaments and photographs.

My own room is very brightly coloured and I have made it very comfortable. The colours I like are yellow and peach and nearly everything in my room is in these colours. I have floral curtains and a floral bedspread. I have a few ornaments and a few photographs. I have my record player and my books. I spend most of my life in this room and I am happy here. In this block there are no bars on the windows because the glass is unbreakable. For the first time in nearly twenty-five years, no bars on the windows. I have turned this room into a home, but not all the patients do. Some leave their rooms completely bare and leave the hospital-issue bedding on their beds. It's as if they are refusing to accept that the hospital is their long-term home. But it is, of course, it is. Some patients cover the walls of their rooms with photographs, usually of nude women or young boys, but I do not choose to do this.

There is more room to move about on this new ward and the paintwork is bright and clean. There are two television rooms, one in the dining room where you can go for a smoke and a chat, and the other is in a special room which is just for watching the TV. There is also a quiet room, where you can read or just sit and think, and a games room with a snooker table, a table tennis table, a games computer, and a radio and cassette machine. I don't bother much with this room. All of us like this ward and our rooms but we are told that if we misbehave the rooms will be taken from us and we will be given smaller ones, and for any bad misbehaviour we will be moved back to the old blocks.

Another reason we don't want to move back is that in this new ward we have our own laundry with washing and drying machines, and a good shower and bathroom. It's not like life on the outside, of course, it can never be that, but it's a thousand times better than what we had. Now I expect some people on the outside, including MPs, will be saying what I have described is too much for madmen, that they are making life too soft for us. Believe me, although our surroundings are better, life in Broadmoor is as tough as it ever was. It is a hard place to be.

As recently as 1988, the Health Advisory Service compiled a report on Broadmoor which condemned the hospital. It said that changes should be made on 256 separate issues, ranging from the management and day-to-day running of the hospital to more effective ways of treating and rehabilitating patients. The report was concerned about the widespread use of drugs on patients by doctors and nurses, and that concern has been repeated in recent television documentaries. One, in 1993, exposed a doctor here who – it was claimed – has bullied patients and carried out drug experiments on them. Some of his male patients even started to grow female breasts. Three patients have died in drug-related incidents in the past seven years. An inquest on a patient called Orville Blackwood heard how he died within three minutes of being given a drug to control his behaviour. Blackwood, who was suffering from schizophrenia and depression, was given the drug when he became violent on Abingdon ward. The pathologist said he did not believe that Blackwood died from natural causes; he said his death was due to heart failure caused by phenothiazines, calming drugs.

The fact is, a hospital like Broadmoor cannot do without drugs. The question is, are too many used? And too often? Sadly, drugs make life worth living for many of the patients here, and I know that they have made my life more controllable. Forget the newspaper stories, though, about drugs being brought in from outside, by patients' visitors, in massive quantities. That doesn't happen any more. Ignore stupid tabloid stories about male and female patients having sex orgies. There is no daily contact at all between male and female patients. We are almost totally segregated: the only time there is ever any contact is at occasional dances, but these are strictly supervised and there is no sexual contact. All the same, one or two hospital romances have started at these dances, and ended in marriage. I don't go to these dances. I hate enforced gaiety.

I have been married twice, nearly three times. Just before we went down in 1969, I almost married a girl I knew in the East End. We were good friends and we thought it would be nice to get married, but Reg's and my life sentence put an end to that. I have always enjoyed the company of women, I like them. Both of my marriages have been in Broadmoor. The first was to a woman called Elaine Mildener, who had two lovely children, a boy and a girl. She started writing to me as a penfriend. Lots of women have written to me over the years, some of them find people like me interesting, I don't know why. Anyway, she started coming to visit me in Broadmoor, and I liked her, we got on well. She wasn't really glamorous, but she was a nice lady. After we were married, though, she got a lot of publicity in the papers, which she didn't like, and it wasn't good for her kids. So she stopped coming to see me. I understood, and we were divorced. I like the feeling of being married, it gives you a feeling of security. And if ever the authorities are considering releasing a patient they like to know he has a steady wife and a comfortable home to go to. My second marriage was to Kate, the woman who is still my wife. I fell in love with her as soon as I saw her. She had been writing to my brother Reg before she started writing to me. She sent me photographs and I could see she was very attractive. Finally, she came to visit me.

She is a very attractive woman but I love her most because of her lovely personality. She is very much like my mother and she makes me laugh. She understands when I am going into one. She has been under a lot of pressure herself because she is married to me, but she handles it well. There is no sex between us, because that is not allowed, but one day I hope there will be. I have never made any secret that I am bisexual. I have liked other men but I am also attracted to women. Why would a woman like Kate marry a man like me? I don't know, you'd better ask her. But it is a fact that many women find the patients here attractive. A lot of women even write to and visit Peter Sutcliffe.

Apart from Kate and my brother Reg, my best friend is a patient here called Charlie Smith. He is in for two murders, but they were committed while he was under the influence of drugs, and a kinder feller it would be impossible to know. There is a good chance he will be released before long and I hope it happens, because he is still young enough to make something of his life. He is a brilliant guitar player and with the help of a good friend of ours on the outside, a young record producer called Scott Pine, he recorded an album of his own songs, called *Caught In Time*. Charlie wrote the songs and sang them into a tape recorder in his room in Somerset House. Scott took them away and put the rest of the backing on in a recording studio. It was very good. Both Charlie and I were very upset when Scott died in 1991, and the Broadmoor authorities showed compassion when they let Charlie go to his funeral.

One of the things that makes Charlie Smith special is that he cares about other patients. Even though he has problems of his own, he makes time for others and tries to help them with their problems. One he befriended was an old feller called George, who'd been here for thirty-five years before cancer killed him. George used to grow tomatoes the size of cricket balls and they were really good to eat. Whenever you met him, George always swore blind he'd been fitted up by the FBI, the CIA, MI5, the KGB and every government agency he could think of. It wasn't what he said but the way he said it, and every time he told his story it would be different. If you didn't know he was insane you could easily have been convinced he'd been framed. But, as Charlie says, did anyone ever bother to check George's story? Maybe it wasn't beyond the realms of possibility, and it has happened before. The author of *Midnight Express* knows only too well what can happen to people in the hands of corrupt officials.

So, this is my life and, in my way, I am happy with it. As happy as I can be. My philosophy is this. I believe we are all just like actors on a stage. We are each given parts to play, and we have to play them to the best of our ability. We may not like the role we have been given, but we mustn't grumble about it; it is not up to us to question the part that has been given us. Look around, you will find there are people with worse parts to play, and others with better parts. But we must see it through to the end, to the evening of life, until the sun goes down – and hope for a worthy ovation. We must consider the other actors on the stage, our friends and the people we love. Even the people we hate. We must not take for granted the good things about ourselves that God has given us, and the beauty of the things around us for all of us to see. 'There is none so blind as those who will not see, and none so deaf as those who will not hear.' Those are my sincere beliefs. The beliefs of the Lifer.

> The years roll by.
> You can see the winter turn
> To summer by the sky.
> Home seems far away.
> How much longer within these walls must I stay?
>
> I say a prayer for my fellow men behind bars
> Who gaze up to freedom at the stars.
> We think things are bad for us,
> But there are crippled children who make no fuss.
>
> Let us awaken from our sleep
> And be as free as sheep.
> Let our hearts soar high,
> As high as birds in the sky.
> As we think of being free,
> As at long last the end of the road
> We can see.

And I would ask you to think about the words of a poem I wrote about Broadmoor. I called it 'The Troubled Mind'.

> As I walk along the Broadmoor corridors
> I see my fellow men trudging the floors
> Getting nowhere, like a boat with no oars.
>
> They all have a troubled mind
> Most are looking for the peace of mind
> They cannot find.
> Some are cruel, some are kind.

God forgive them who have the troubled mind.
Only when they go to the Great Beyond
Peace will they find.

CHAPTER SEVEN

Kate's Story

My name is Kate. I am thirty-five. I am a divorcée who's never had children.

I'm not boasting, but I think I am attractive, quite intelligent, fairly amusing, with a bit of a bubbly personality. I have a good figure and I dress well. I live on my own in a nice flat in a town in Kent, and I drive a BMW. I have been involved in various business ventures over the years, including a kissogram company, and achieved success.

I have never been a notorious sort of person. I have never made newspaper headlines. I never expected to and I never wanted to. But, none the less, I did. Because I am the woman who married Ronnie Kray. I am the lady who really did say, 'I do, Ron, Ron. I do.' And I'm not kidding!

Sometimes, I'll be honest, I find it hard to believe myself what has happened. But it's a fact. For better or for worse – and often it's been for worse – I have been Ron's wife since 7 November 1989. And, as I write, I am still Mrs Kray. In that time I've known laughter, tears, bitterness and happiness. Sometimes, when I see silly headlines in newspapers, like 'Blonde tells of her love for Mad Ronnie' and 'I stole Ronnie Kray's heart with laughter', I still find it difficult to believe it's me they are writing about.

I first became involved with the Krays in 1987. How it came about was really strange, though I knew from an early age that I would have a long association with a prison or someone in a prison. I don't know how I knew that but I always did, it was like a premonition I had inside me.

It all started at the end of a day's shopping in London. I had just missed my train home to Kent and, while I waited for the next train, I thought I'd have a look at the books and magazines at one of the bookstalls on Charing Cross station. I've never really been a great book reader, I've never seemed to have the time and I don't think I've ever bought a book for myself in my whole life. For some reason I found myself looking at the books in the crime section and one book seemed to catch my attention. It was called *The Profession of Violence* by John Pearson. Perhaps it was the photograph on the front of the book which held my attention – a photograph of two rather grim-looking young men. I picked up the book and started flicking through the pages and saw some more pictures of these same young men. They were, of course, the Kray twins. I'd heard of them but I didn't really know much about them. To this day I still don't know why but I felt compelled to buy the book. I also bought a couple of magazines and it was them that I read on the journey home. I put the book in my bag and forgot all about it. It stayed there for about three months and then, one day, I found it again and started to read it. I found that I couldn't put it down, I was completely enthralled by this story of Reggie and Ronnie Kray. I just found them fascinating characters.

When I finished the book I felt I just had to write to Reggie Kray, to tell him how much I had enjoyed reading about his life, to find out what had happened to him since he was imprisoned. Don't ask me why I felt like this, I've never done anything remotely like it before. I've never felt compelled to write a letter to a complete stranger, especially someone like him, but it just seemed the most natural thing for me to do. I wasn't lonely, I wasn't a weirdo and I certainly wasn't any kind of 'groupie'. I still can't really explain what made me do it. Anyway, I rang a newspaper and discovered that Reggie was still in prison – at Gartree, near Market Harborough, in Leicestershire. Then I sat down and started to write.

Looking back on it now I suppose my letter must have seemed a bit dumb. In it I told him about reading the book and how I wondered what had happened to him since. Because I wasn't quite sure what else to write I asked him daft things, like had his hair gone grey now round the 'Shirleys' (temples) and did he still have his own teeth! Really daft things, just trying to be amusing, I suppose. I also sent him a photograph of myself so that he could see I wasn't some old dragon who was writing to him. I honestly never expected to get a reply but I'll never forget it when I did. His letter arrived on my birthday and I was chuffed to bits.

We wrote to each other for about four months, at least one letter every week. He turned out to be a prolific letter-writer though I sometimes found his writing hard to decipher. It was very squiggly and scrawly, as though he'd got a thousand things on his mind and he was rushing to get them all down, and he was clearly a bad sleeper because he told me that he wrote many of his letters in the early hours of the morning. He told me about his daily routine in prison, the people he'd met, and how he'd spent the years since he was sent to prison. He told me about the things he liked, music and so on, and he also mentioned his twin brother, Ron, a lot. He was obviously very fond of him. He told me Ron was at Broadmoor. I knew it was a special hospital for criminals but I didn't know much more than that. I wasn't even sure where Broadmoor was. He also asked me lots of questions about myself.

I wrote to him about my life which must have seemed pretty

tame compared to his. I told him how I'd been born Kathleen Anne Reville, on 11 June 1956. That makes me a Gemini, the sign of the twins, which, I suppose, was another omen. My dad was Irish and my mother a half-caste. My dad is a carpenter and my mother has worked in the same factory for twenty-three years. I had an ordinary enough childhood for the neighbourhood in which I was brought up. Times were a bit hard for my parents so I was brought up in a large boarding house, in Dartford, Kent, with my nan and grandad and their eleven children. My nan was half black so we were called 'those little Woggie West kids.' I don't know why but as it was never said viciously it never really worried or upset me.

In any case we were all too busy trying to survive to worry about people calling us names. We never had much as kids and I remember always wearing hand-me-downs from other kids. We never had new clothes of our own. And it wasn't until years later that I discovered it was the norm to have milk on cornflakes and not boiling water. But what my grandparents lacked in money and material things they tried to make up with kindness.

They were great story-tellers and used to enthrall me when they told me about the history of the family, which seemed to me to be very dramatic. They told me that, at the time of the Civil War in America, there was a big uprising in Alabama, which was where my great-grandfather – my grandmother's father – was born. My great-grandfather was only three years old at the time and his father hid him on a ship while he went back to collect the rest of his family, so that they could escape the uprising. Well, he never returned and the ship – the *Princess Alice* – sailed with the little boy still hidden on board. Finally he was discovered but as it was too late to turn back the crew looked after him and the captain, who was called Johnnie, took a liking to the little black boy and named him Johnnie Alice.

He eventually arrived in Portsmouth, was 'adopted' by a woman who ran a whorehouse in the port, and grew up quite happily there. When he was older he had four children, one of whom was my nan. I used to love listening to this and other stories that my grandparents told me. Life was a bit chaotic when I was young because I also had two brothers and a sister and my nan was still having children while I was growing up. I've even got an uncle who is younger than me!

I did have a problem when I was about six years old, when a friend of the family offered to take me and my younger brother on an outing. I remember he made my brother wait and turn his back while he took me into some bushes and tried to molest me. I can remember being very frightened and I ran out of the bushes, grabbed my brother's hand and we ran home together. I was too scared to tell either my parents or my grandparents. I later learned that this same man had been sent to prison for molesting a child.

When I was eleven years old I met two boys, one of whom I was later to marry. I was married for the first time when I was sixteen. I was pregnant at the time and had an abortion which was done badly. I got peritonitis because of this which, I later discovered, had left me infertile. It wasn't that I was promiscuous, I think I was just terribly ignorant. No one had ever bothered to explain the facts of life to me. I had to learn the hard way about sex and men.

My first marriage lasted only a year and a day. I can remember the wedding vividly. It was on 1 June and I had a big white wedding with as many trimmings as we could afford at the time. He wasn't a bad boy, he meant well, but I can recall walking in the back door of his mum's house, where we were living, three months after the marriage. He was sitting at the kitchen table wearing a pair of pink striped pyjamas and smoking a pipe. I thought to myself, 'God, is this what it's going to be like for the rest of my life?' That was really the beginning of the end of that marriage. Needless to say it didn't last a lot longer. I finally told him it was all over and, as I left, he said to me, 'I hope you find what you're looking for.' Well, I can honestly say a man in pink pyjamas smoking a pipe wasn't it!

When I left I carried my suitcase home to my mum's because that's where I felt I wanted to be. I guess I just wanted a bit of love and some home comforts. But she was not sympathetic. As I arrived at her doorstep she told me, 'Sod off!' She said, 'You made your bed, now lie on it.' I suppose she was trying to make me give my marriage another go. Instead I went to see my brother, Joe, and he offered to put me up at the house he shared with his wife and two children. Unfortunately, while I was there, because I was so down in the dumps and unsure of what the future held for me, I started drinking heavily and got myself in a right old mess. It wasn't until I got really sick that my dad came and got me and took me home. I have never drunk alcohol since.

I can remember the lovely feeling of being home. I had a hot bath and sat in front of the fire and I felt really safe and warm. It was a brilliant feeling. Soon I started to get myself together and I managed to find a job at a swimming pool as a lifeguard. I'd always been a good swimmer and I started studying in my spare time to be a swimming teacher. I passed all my exams and started giving swimming lessons to adults on my evenings off. Everything was fine again, until one day during a long, hot summer. By then I was in my twenties and I knew I'd developed into quite an attractive girl.

This particular day was especially hot. I'd just got home from my afternoon shift at the pool and a few of us decided to go for a swim. We had a nice time but as the evening wore on my friends all began to leave and go home. The only people left were me and this one particular man.

There had never been anything improper between us before, not even the suggestion of it, but suddenly and without warning he hit me over the head with a rock and put his hands around my throat as if he was going to strangle me. Then, violently, he tried to rape me. I fought him off and he failed in his attempt. But I can honestly say I have never got over what he tried to do to me. Even though later he cried and said sorry, when you trust someone and they break that trust, you find it very hard to trust a man again. I figured that if I couldn't trust him, a friend, then I couldn't trust any man. They always say it's the person you least expect and, in my case, that was true. But then I met Harry, the boy I had known when I was just eleven. But, if I'd changed, boy! so had he. Now he was a real Flash Harry! He looked really good in his handmade suits and crocodile shoes. I'd always liked him, all those years ago, and we found we were getting on really well once again. We started going out together and I loved him because he was funny and he made me laugh. He had his own flat and eventually I moved in with him. He supported me all the way with my studies because he knew how desperate I was to get on, to better myself. He once told me there wasn't *anything* I couldn't do if I put my mind to it. And he was right. With his help I worked really hard and we began to build a good life. He asked me to marry him and I said yes.

It wasn't long before we bought our first house in Maidstone, Kent. The happy ending to the story, I suppose, would have come if we'd had kids, but I couldn't have children because of the bad abortion I'd had when I was sixteen so Harry and I buried ourselves in work instead. We tried all sorts of businesses knowing that one day we'd come up with a real winner. And we did. It was a kissogram business, which we called Kandy's. I did a lot of the actual kissogram work myself and I was good at it. Now, most men would get all funny and say, 'I'm not letting my wife do that sort of thing,' but not Harry, he knew he could trust me. We were very successful and soon we bought a big house in the country. Then we opened a shop called Flash Harry's, selling men's clothes and, again, it did well.

We were working day and night and I got tired and close to exhaustion. Harry realized and took me on holiday to the Canary Islands. It was the best surprise I'd ever had. After we returned we invested in property and letting bed-sits and we continued to do well. But, sadly, all the hours we were working began to take their toll on our marriage and slowly we began to grow apart. By this time we had been married thirteen years and we'd rarely had an argument in all that time. Neither of us wanted to get to the stage where we did start to fall out and dislike each other – so we decided to get a divorce. We're still partners in the business sense, still the best of friends, and I still love him very dearly. I truly hope that one day he meets the person who is right for him and who will give him the family that I couldn't. He is a good man.

And that's the position in my life that I had reached when I saw that book on the Krays and started to write to Reggie. Finally, after about four months of writing he asked me to go and visit him at Gartree prison. I was really nervous on the long journey up from Kent to Market Harborough. The prison is a grim-looking set of buildings in the middle of what seems to be mile upon mile of flat fields, two or three miles outside the town. I'd never been to a prison before and, the first time I went to one I found it to be quite an unnerving experience. I went into a small reception area and my name was checked off by a prison officer against a list of expected visitors. It was all very formal and the officer told me to go and wait until the name of the prisoner I was visiting was called out.

Several other women were there, some with children, all waiting to visit other prisoners. The atmosphere was very subdued and there was no conversation. Finally a voice shouted, 'Visitor for Kray.' I walked forward to an iron door, I heard a key turning in the lock on the other side and the door opened. I went into another room and had to go through a metal-detection gate to see if I was carrying any metal objects. While this was happening an officer was checking through my handbag. Then it was through another door and into the visiting hall. Actually it was more like a shed, very bleak and barren, with lots of formica-covered tables and chairs.

I thought I would be meeting Reggie here but an officer in the hall indicated that I should go to a small room at the end of the hall. I learned later that prisoners can request this room if they have a 'special' visitor coming and want to talk a little more privately. In this room was a table and two chairs. I sat down, my mind buzzing. What would we say to each other? What would be my first words? What would he say to me? What would he be like? I waited for what seemed like ages but was really only a few minutes when the door opened and in walked Reggie Kray. I recognized him immediately, I knew it had to be him.

The first words he said to me were, 'Better shut that door.'

'Oh,' I said, 'you sound just like Larry Grayson's Everard.'

We both cracked up laughing and that broke the ice. From that moment we got on like a house on fire, chatting non-stop. I felt as if I had known him for years. And yes, he was grey round the 'Shirleys', and yes, he did have all his own teeth! He was smaller than I'd expected but very muscular and fit-looking, very fast-talking and full of a kind of explosive nervous energy.

We talked about his life in Gartree, how much better it was than Parkhurst, on the Isle of Wight, where he'd spent so many years, even though Gartree was by no means a 'soft' prison. He told me a bit about his mother and about his brother, Ron, and I remember him saying, 'I'm not a bad man and neither is Ron, yet we've been banged up for so many years now. It doesn't really seem fair, Kate, but we've just got to put up with it.'

That was really the start of our friendship and I continued to write to and visit Reg as often as possible. It was not a romantic thing, it was purely friendship. He told me all about his wife, who had died, and how he would never get involved romantically with another woman out of respect to her memory. But we kept in regular touch and all through that time he kept urging me to go and visit Ron in Broadmoor. I kept trying to put him off. I thought Broadmoor must be an eerie place and I suppose I was frightened of the unknown, scared by Broadmoor's reputation. Broadmoor Hospital for the Criminally Insane. Just saying those words sent a shiver down my spine. Later I was to find out how wrong I was and what a caring place it is.

Ron once said to me, 'This place can be heaven or hell, it all depends on you.' And that just about sums it up, really. I suppose, also, I was nervous of getting in touch with Ron because of what I had read about his so-called 'madness'. Contacting and meeting Reggie was one thing . . . but Ronnie? Well, I just wasn't sure about it at all.

Anyway, I started writing to him. His letters back to me were much shorter than Reg's. I thought at first that this was because he didn't really want to write to me but later I discovered that Ron simply doesn't enjoy writing letters. Finally he wrote and asked me if I would go and visit him the following week. I thought about it. I didn't really want to go, but how could I say no?

I drove up to Broadmoor and sat for quite a while in the car park outside. I looked at the walls and the bleak, dark buildings and I thought to myself, 'God, I can't go in there.' Even outside there's an atmosphere about the place: it's quiet, sort of unsettled, disturbed, like something could happen at any moment. But I plucked up courage and walked into the reception area.

I told them who I was, who I'd come to see and signed my name in a large book. Then I just stood around and waited. Finally my name was called by an officer and I followed him through several doors which were locked shut behind me. Then along some corridors, all painted a dreadful yellow colour, until we reached what I can only describe as a school assembly hall, because that's what it looked like. It was a big room, full of tables and chairs, and it had a big stage running along one side of it. This was the visiting room.

It was quiet and cold in there and quite smoky. I noticed several more officers – actually they are called nurses, though I didn't realize that at the time – some male and some female. All of them looked at me, obviously wondering who this blonde lady was and who she'd come to see. Sat by himself at a table in the middle of the room was a smartly dressed man. He looked at me, I looked at him – and straight away I realized that this was Ronnie Kray.

My first impression was, 'Bloody hell, he looks like a bank manager!' He was dressed in a navy blue double-breasted suit, a white double-cuffed shirt, a smart tie and beautifully polished black shoes. He looked smashing! For some reason I'd never expected him to be wearing a suit. Whenever I'd met Reg he was usually in a grey tracksuit and always in casual clothing.

Ronnie shook my hand, kissed me gently on the cheek, and we sat down. He asked me if I wanted tea or coffee. Then there was a lull in the conversation as we took stock of each other. I thought he was a bit older-looking than I'd expected and he was wearing spectacles. He was very softly spoken and very polite. He said to me, 'Kate, you look wonderful.'

And, at that moment, I really felt as though I did.

I had a pot of coffee and Ron had a six-pack of non-alcohol lager served by a 'waiter' in a white jacket who, he explained, was another patient who did the job for a small payment. He told me that many patients in the hospital had jobs which paid them a bit of money to buy cigarettes and chocolate and other little luxuries, but that he had never had a job in all the years he had been there. He asked me lots of questions about me, but really I wanted to talk to him about the things he liked. He told me how he loved classical music and how he listened to it in his room every day, how he enjoyed reading books, and how he had just one close friend in the whole place, a patient called Charlie Smith, a much younger man than him, who was in Broadmoor for murder committed when he was under the influence of drugs. He told me that Charlie was a very gentle man who was also a good guitarist, and he would sometimes play his guitar and sing songs to Ron. I found it hard, listening to him talk like this, to believe that this was the same man I had first read about in that book, who had committed all those crimes and who the newspapers painted as a really evil man.

That was the only time he got a bit aggravated in our whole conversation, when he spoke about what some of the papers write about him. How they said he lived a life of luxury in the hospital when, in reality, he had no extra privileges and was, in fact, more restricted than most of the other patients. He wasn't even allowed to walk around the hospital grounds and gardens.

We had a really nice conversation which lasted for about two hours. I must say, I liked him and I was impressed by him. He was nothing like I had expected. The only thing I wasn't too keen on was that he seemed to smoke a lot but, I thought to myself, he's got to have some pleasure in life. At the end of our meeting he got up, shook my hand, kissed me again on the cheek and said, 'Please come and see me again, Kate.' I stood and watched as he was led away by a nurse and he gave me a wave.

In the week which followed he sent me a beautiful bouquet of flowers, then came a letter asking me to go and see him again a couple of weeks later. On this next occasion we again had a nice conversation, though he seemed a bit agitated, as if he'd got something on his mind. Finally, he came out with it. Right out of the blue he said to me, 'If you don't marry Reggie, will you marry me?'

God, I thought to myself, this man has got more 'front' than Woolworths! I was, to say the least, shocked. Especially when I saw from the expression on his face that he wasn't joking. Reggie and I had no intention of getting married; we were just friends, nothing else. I told Ron this and, as gently as possible, I told him that marriage was the last thing on my mind. He seemed to accept this, though he didn't seem too pleased about it.

After I left Ron on that second visit I honestly thought that might be the end of our friendship. I thought I'd probably offended him and wouldn't ever hear from him again. I didn't know then that he's one of the most persistent men in the world and never takes no for an answer! I hoped I wouldn't lose him as a friend but there really was no way I was ever going to get married again . . . to anyone.

However, his letters continued – and so did my visits. Our friendship continued to grow – and so did his marriage proposals. Every time I went to see him he asked me to marry him. Finally,

in the early summer of 1989, I said yes. Don't ask me why I
changed my mind, it just seemed the right thing to do. Over a
period of time I just found myself thinking that he was the perfect
man for me, that I liked pretty well everything about him, that I
was in love with him. He was so pleased when I agreed to get
married, and must have got the news telephoned to Reg straight
away because a day or so later I received a letter from Reg saying
how pleased *he* was, how we had his blessing, and how I couldn't
have picked a better-looking chap! Ironic really, seeing as how
they are identical twins!

We had a good laugh over that, in fact we had a good laugh
on all my visits because laughter, I feel, is one of the most
important parts of our relationship. And laughter is something
I've always shared with the staff at Broadmoor, who've turned
out to be really nice people, in the main. They always had a smile
for me, and still do, and that makes things pleasant. There has
never been any animosity shown by them to me.

A lot of people seem surprised whenever I talk about Ron
having a great sense of humour. But it's true, he really does, and
he can take a joke against himself. I remember when mad cow
disease started to make all the headlines. I went to see Ron one
morning and he said to me, 'I've decided not to eat beef any
more, Kate, because it drives you mad.'

'But you're mad already, Ron,' I said.

'Oh, yeah, so I am,' he replied, 'at least, that's what they
say. Still, you'd better stop eating it anyway.' And he was roaring
with laughter when he said it.

There was another occasion when one of the highbrow
Sunday newspaper colour supplements had got hold of a painting
which Ron had done and they had got a psychologist to analyse
it. The painting was of a little house, which he often paints. The
psychologist said the red and black sky and the red and black
house in the painting showed that Ron was in a black mood and
prone to acute depression. I asked Ron for his comments. 'What
a load of bollocks,' he said. 'I used red and black because they

were the only colours I'd got left in my paintbox.' Again we had a good laugh. So much for psychology!

But there were serious things to discuss, of course, and one of them was Ron's sexuality. Whenever anyone talks about me and Ron the subject will inevitably get round to sex – or the lack of it. Let me make my own position clear on this. Sex is not all that important to me and it hasn't been for a long time, probably because of those fairly disastrous experiences I had with men when I was much younger. I really am not bothered about it – there are far more important aspects to relationships between men and women.

However, I still had to ask myself, did I want to marry a homosexual, no matter how much I liked or loved him? I put the problem to Ron and I will never forget what he said to me.

He said, 'I am not a homosexual, Kate, I am bisexual. I've always believed in being open about this and I don't believe people should be afraid to admit it, if they have homosexual leanings. It won't make any difference to your friends, not if they are real friends. Some of the greatest men in history have been bisexual and it's nothing to be ashamed of. It's something you are born with, like the colour of your eyes.' And he added, 'I will always be a man as far as you're concerned, Kate, and I will prove that to you, one day.'

That was good enough for me and I knew I could accept him the way he was. In any case, again because of the circumstances he's found himself in, sex is not all that important to Ron any more, either. Anyway, as I've said, by the summer of 1989 I had agreed to become Ron's wife, and it was a decision which would turn my quiet life upside down.

Ron warned me that the news would get out because there's always someone in any special hospital or prison establishment who will leak things to the press. He told me things could start to get difficult for me, and he wasn't kidding. The constant travelling to visit him I could handle but the pressure from newspaper reporters was something else. And, of course, I soon discovered all sorts of opportunist characters creeping out of the woodwork, trying to sell stories and make a few pounds off the backs of me and Ron. But even now, when I weigh it all up, I still think the Colonel has been worth the aggro. There is something between Ron and me that I just can't explain. I simply know it was right, that it was all meant to be.

Once news of our wedding plans was out, all hell broke loose. My own family were marvellous about it. Their attitude was that it was my own business, that I was a grown woman who knew what she wanted and what she was getting herself into. And if marrying Ron was what I wanted, then it was okay by them. My friends were great, too, and so was Harry, who said he would support me all the way. That was typical of him and the loyalty he's always shown to me.

Planning a wedding in Broadmoor is not easy and I knew that our wedding had to be held there because there was no way that Ron would get permission to be married outside the hospital. And against the background of our wedding preparations Ron's divorce from Elaine Mildener, his first wife, was still going through. Theirs had been the first marriage ever allowed inside the hospital but it failed because of the tremendous pressures exerted on her, which I can understand. Ronnie divorced Elaine on the grounds of desertion, which they both agreed to. I've never met Elaine but Ron speaks well of her and I admire her, and I wish her and her family every happiness in the future.

The divorce story appeared in some of the papers and some of the less scrupulous tabloids started carrying stories about the so-called 'other women' in Ron's life. In fact, there hadn't been any other women, not romantically speaking, just lots of friends. You see, that's the thing about Ron and Reg, they have so many friends. When I agreed to marry Ron he gave me a book full of the names and addresses and phone numbers of all his friends. There were dozens of them and he said, 'They're my friends, Kate, and now they're your friends as well.'

Other newspapers started carrying 'exclusive' stories from

people who claimed to have previously untold stories of life with the Kray twins when they ruled London's underworld. Some of the claims were really outrageous and could have really upset Ron. But, once again, the ability to have a laugh and a joke about what was written gave us the strength to see it through. I'll give you an example. One Sunday paper carried an article by a midget who claimed he had once been a hit man for the Krays. Ron hardly knew the man and was angry about the article. So I said to him, 'What did the dwarf specialize in, Ron? Was it knee-capping jobs? Not a good choice of unobtrusive hit man, Ron . . . not too many gun-toting dwarfs walking around!'

Ron saw the funny side of it. Once again, humour had saved the day. I don't want to be critical of all of the newspapers, though. I think, for example, the *Sun* got it right with two of their headlines in November, 1989: 'Kate stole Ronnie Kray's heart with laughter', and 'Bride Kate keeps him smiling in Broadmoor'.

We'd set our wedding date for 6 November 1989, and in the weeks leading up to the wedding the media attention became almost impossible. I had reporters almost literally camped outside my front door. I talked to Ron about it and he said it would be for the best if I agreed to give some interviews. I was nervous about this because I had never done it before, but I thought that I had got nothing to hide and nothing to be ashamed of, and maybe if I did some interviews the press would get off my back. It didn't work out that way, of course, but I did start giving interviews, some of which were reported fairly and others which weren't.

I also went on television, which again is an ordeal for anyone who's experiencing it for the first time. I went on Derek Jameson's chat show on Sky Television. He tried to get me going on Ron being a homosexual, but I wasn't going to get drawn into any of that nonsense. I don't claim that I outsmarted Mr Jameson but I like to think he realized I'm not the dumb blonde that I might look. I also did an interview for a London Weekend

Television programme which was filmed. Their interviewer suggested that I was marrying Ron for his money. But that must have looked a bit daft, seeing as how Ron didn't have any and the interview was done in the back of *my* gold Rolls-Royce! Just before the wedding I also did an interview with the TVS programme *Coast to Coast* which they shot in a marina in Southampton. That was the best one of the lot because they managed to get a bit of humour into it, as well as the more serious stuff.

Some of the women's magazines couldn't resist joining in all the hype. You know the sort of articles, 'Why does an attractive 33-year-old blonde [their words] want to get married to a 55-year-old gangster serving a minimum of thirty years for murder?' And then they would get some so-called marriage expert to analyse my motives. All the 'experts' had different views but along similar lines: she had a deprived childhood, she's looking for a father figure, she's looking for attention, she's seeking notoriety. Not one of them seemed to consider for a moment that I might just have fallen in love.

One 'expert' said I was looking for the security of marriage without all the 'messy bits' such as washing his socks and underpants and having to go to bed with him. Another writer even had the cheek to ask, 'Aren't you afraid you'll catch Aids?' The answer to that is no, I'm not. Because neither of us has it and both of us are faithful to each other.

The magazines are still at it, even now. Only recently I saw a psychologist saying of women who visit male prisoners: 'There's an element of eroticism. Fear and danger are sexual stimuli for some people. That's why some women are drawn irrevocably to the most dangerous, tough and violent men. They represent masculinity at its crudest and most raw.' Honestly, Ron isn't dangerous and he isn't violent, but of course he's tough. I wouldn't want a man any other way. Anyway, that's all I really want to say on this subject. Let's get back to that upcoming wedding which was causing so much commotion.

Our biggest problem, all along, had been to get the Broadmoor authorities to give us their permission. Without it there would be no marriage and I would have to continue my life being plain Kate Howard. It was important to demonstrate to the authorities that we were absolutely sincere in our feelings for each other, that this wasn't just a 'flash in the pan'.

I had to go and see Dr Ferris, Ron's specialist at Broadmoor, on several occasions. He explained to me that Ron is a chronic paranoid schizophrenic. He has an illness of the mind which can cause fairly quick and dramatic changes of mood, but it can be completely controlled by medication. He told me that Ron is not a dangerous person any more, nor is he ever likely to be again. His problems have been identified, they have subsided greatly over the years and, as long as he has his drugs, his future problems will be relatively minimal.

None the less, Dr Ferris explained, marriage to a man like Ron would be a hard task for any woman to undertake. There would be an enormous amount of strain and worry and the stress of trying to maintain a relationship with a partner who is locked away. However, he also told me that he felt Ron would be curable in time and could, eventually, be released from Broadmoor. His first step would probably be to a less restricted hospital but he could even, in time, be released into a home environment, albeit under supervision. But he made it clear that there were no guarantees and, in any case, he was talking in the long term.

He also put my mind – and Ron's – at rest by emphasizing that Ron would never be sent back into a prison environment because he would not be able to cope with it any more. That's always been Ron's biggest worry, that he would be sent back to somewhere like Parkhurst where they wouldn't understand his problems and where life can be cruel and stressful to anyone who isn't fit and well. Dr Ferris said he'd had discussions with Alan Franey, Broadmoor's general manager, and they would give permission for our marriage – but he urged me to think again carefully before taking such a big step. To think not only about my feelings but also about Ron's because his progress could be harmed if the marriage failed to survive.

Well, I did think about it, long and hard. Ron and I spoke about it at length and we both agreed. We *did* want to get married and we *did* sincerely believe we could make it work. I told Dr Ferris this and I was pleased when he said he would give us his blessing. Ronnie was over the moon about it all, even more so when his divorce went through without any problems. We'd set the date for 6 November after meeting the chaplain at Broadmoor, who said he'd be pleased to officiate at the ceremony. Then I went and saw Terry, the catering manager at the hospital, and he said he'd take care of all the arrangements for food and drink and so on. 'You can have what you like,' he told me, 'as long as you pay for it.' Well, you can't say fairer than that!

I saw Mr Franey who told me we would be allowed eight guests for the wedding. Ronnie said he wanted Reggie to come and also Charlie Richardson who, with his brother, had run their gang in south London at the same time as the Krays had ruled east London. At the time, of course, they'd not been good friends but time is a great healer and over the years they'd met up in various prisons and found they got on very well. It had always been 'business' between them, anyway, according to Ron, never 'personal'. And when Charlie Richardson got out of prison he started visiting Ron at Broadmoor. They'd become really good friends over the years and Ron wanted Charlie to come to the wedding. But the authorities weren't keen and blocked it.

Reggie was a different story. The prison authorities said it would be okay for him to be sent down from Gartree for the wedding, but then Reg got the 'hump' after a disagreement he'd had with Ron. It was nothing, really, just one of those silly little squabbles you get in all families. Anyway, Reg said he wouldn't come, then changed his mind – but by then the Home Office said it was too late to make the necessary travel arrangements, so Reggie couldn't come. Ronnie was upset about this because he thinks a lot of Reg, but we were determined it wasn't going to spoil our big day.

In the end the eight guests were my best friend, Sharon Denley, who agreed to be my maid of honour, Ronnie's older brother, Charlie, and five men who'd been close to Ron for many years – Joe Pyle, Alex Stein, Wilf Pine, Paul Lake, the artist, and Charlie Smith, Ron's best friend who was to be the best man. To take the photographs Ron wanted David Bailey, the society photographer who'd taken the pictures at Reggie's wedding all those years ago and who had taken some of the best photographs of the twins when they were at their peak. Unfortunately, he was working out of the country and couldn't make it, so we had to make do with a local photographer who did the job brilliantly and took some lovely photographs.

To make it up to me for the fact that David Bailey couldn't take the photographs Ron arranged for me to have a photo session with Lord Lichfield, the Queen's cousin and probably the most famous photographer in the world, at his studios in London. It must have cost Ron an arm and a leg – I didn't dare ask how much! – but I was pleased with the results. As a matter of fact Lord Lichfield's photographs were so good I had a job recognizing myself! And he turned out to be a really charming man who put me completely at my ease. No false airs or graces at all. Ronnie even went to the trouble of buying all the copyrights on the photos so that they belonged to me completely and wouldn't fall into the wrong hands and start turning up in newspapers and magazines all over the world. He thinks of everything, that man.

Having my photo taken by Lord Lichfield wasn't strictly necessary, I know, but it was a nice touch to add to the most special day in my life.

I bought a beautiful dress for the wedding and I got a tailor at Maidstone called Dennis Courtman to make Ron a smashing wedding suit, plus five other suits for him. I also bought him a magnificent gold watch. Ronnie bought me a gold Cartier engagement ring, studded with thirty pure white diamonds, and a wedding ring made with a circle of rubies and diamonds. He also gave me his gold signet ring with the initials RK engraved on it. I tell you, he's the most generous man in the world. If he likes you, Ron would give you his last penny. In fact, on more than one occasion he *has* given away more or less his last penny to friends who've been down on their luck. Often he gives money away to people he doesn't even know just because he feels sorry for them. He really isn't the hard-hearted villain so many people make him out to be.

I will never forget the morning of my wedding day. I looked out of my bedroom window and the front garden was full of reporters and photographers. Harry, my ex-husband, managed to keep them all at bay and how I would have managed without him I just don't know. I collected my friend, Sharon, and we had a leisurely drive up to the Hilton Hotel at Bracknell, which is not far from Broadmoor. That was where a party had been organized for many of Ron's friends after the wedding and I was going to spend the night there before going to see Ron the next day.

I got myself dressed and made up, Sharon did my hair, and then we drove to the hospital. I was so nervous I thought I might not be able to go through with it and things weren't helped when we arrived at Broadmoor and saw all the photographers and television crews with their lights. We arrived at the hospital at about four fifteen and the wedding was due to take place exactly one hour later. Sharon and I were eventually taken to the chapel and Ronnie was stood at the altar waiting for me. He looked the best I had ever seen him. He squeezed my hand and gave me a kiss and when he saw how nervous I was he tried to make me laugh. He told me that when the chaplain asked him, 'Do you take this woman to be your lawful wedded wife?', he was going to throw himself on the floor, shouting, 'Don't be silly, I'm not that mad, am I?'

He was calm, collected and very reassuring. He kept giving me quiet smiles. The whole wedding ceremony, for me, was a complete blur, though I had a job to stop myself from crying. It was all very moving and emotional and it was lovely having people around Ron who obviously cared for him very much. Charlie Smith was a smashing best man and he gave us a wonderful wedding gift. He paid for the reception at Broadmoor – and what a reception it was. We had lobster, fresh salmon, caviar, champagne and a lovely two-tiered, heart-shaped wedding cake which had been made in the kitchens at Broadmoor. There were a hundred pink and white balloons hanging from the ceiling, with trailing ribbons, and garlands of flowers everywhere.

I so wanted the occasion to be special because this, for Ron, was the whole day, they wouldn't let him come to the reception at the Hilton afterwards. And it *was* special, a really lovely occasion that lasted for two hours. Then we had to leave. It was so sad leaving Ron and Charlie behind but, typical of my Ronnie, he just said, 'Go and enjoy yourself, Kate.' So off I went, leaving my new husband behind. I was really upset.

When I got back to the hotel I was really drained but I was in for another shock. There had been a lot of cameras as we drove away from Broadmoor but there were even more waiting for us at the hotel. It was nerve-racking but, give the reporters and photographers their due, once they'd got their quotes and their pictures, they agreed to go away and leave us alone. Then I went into my second reception of the evening and met all of Ron's long-standing friends. There must have been at least two hundred of them. They were very kind to me and made me feel really special, and we all drank a toast to an absent friend.

Now, every night at eight o'clock I always phone Ron and this night was to be no exception. I'm never allowed to talk directly to him, just to pass a message on via the nurse on duty on his ward. Well, at eight o'clock I made my excuses to the guests at the party and went to my room to call Ron as usual. It made me laugh when the nurse on duty called out, 'Ron, it's your missus on the phone!' I could hear Ronnie laughing in the background.

We had a smashing party at the Hilton but, even though I

was tired, I didn't sleep much after it. I spent most of the night thinking about the events of the day before. By ten o'clock the next morning I was back at Broadmoor to see my husband. It was strange signing the red book 'Mrs Kray' instead of 'Mrs Howard'. It was so good to see him that morning and we had lots to talk about. I will never forget one of the things he said to me. He said that when they took him from the chapel back to his room the night before, they'd had to walk across an open court-yard. It was the first time in twenty-three years that he'd walked under the stars. He couldn't get over the wonder of the experience. Something that we all take completely for granted had meant so much to him. I felt very humble when he told me that. A short walk under the stars at night, something that you and I wouldn't even give a thought to, had meant everything to him.

Since that day I have visited Ron on every possible occasion. Usually I am allowed to see him twice, occasionally three times, a week. Officially he's allowed to have seven midweek visits a month and four visits any weekend which, compared to most prisons, is considered generous. Each visit can last up to two hours. He has his non-alcohol lager, I have coffee, and we sit and talk and talk. We never seem to run out of things to talk about.

We often talk about Ron's young days and his memories of Reg and his family but we rarely talk about when he was a criminal. To me, that was another Ronnie Kray, someone I've read about but a man who bears no resemblance to the man I am now married to. That man was dangerous, they say, but this man isn't. They say he's raving mad, but he isn't. Some say he's stupid, but he isn't. When it comes to business, for example, he's second to none. It says a lot for both of the twins that they've kept themselves going financially all the time they've been locked away – and none of their money, which they've mostly given away, has been earned through any kind of illegal venture. They still donate to untold charities and, in their situation, that takes some doing.

If ever you were to meet and talk to Ron, you would find he's just like you and me, he isn't any different. Then, why is he in Broadmoor? I can hear you asking. Well, I'm not saying that Ron hasn't got a mental illness, because he would be the first to admit that he has. You see, most of the time Ron is 'normal', but every now and then he gets paranoid and feels everything is closing in on him. He calls it 'going into one' and he always knows when it's happening. He's been like this since he was very young and now he always recognizes the signs. He then seeks the relevant help with his medication and he likes to be alone. These periods in his life don't last for long and soon he's back to his old self again. It's at these bad times, though, when I feel useless. I wish I could do something to help him, to take away the pain. It's not a physical pain, it's a mental pain, and that's the worst sort. It's not like a cut leg or a broken arm, something which surgeons can see and heal. The person with a mental problem is a person alone, wrestling with their thoughts, trying to decide what is normal and what is not. I know, from watching Ron, that this is an incredibly lonely time. Sometimes I look at him and I see that he is a very lonely man, even though he can be surrounded by many people and dozens of letters from well-wishers. Even though he has so many friends, so many people who truly care for him, he is still lonely and isolated in his mind.

I now realize that when I first married Ron, despite all the warnings and advice I had been given, I didn't understand just how much my life was about to change. For instance, I am never introduced to people as 'Kate' any more, it's always, 'This is Ronnie Kray's wife.' Then I am always bombarded with questions.

'Which one is it you're married to?' Ronnie, I say.

'Which is the gay one?' My husband, I say.

'Which one is in the nuthouse?' My husband, I say.

People are normally a bit gobsmacked by this time. Then it's always, 'How did you meet him?' Then 'Why did you marry him?'

I don't take offence at these questions because I know people are curious. It seems everybody wants to know about Ronnie and Reggie, from lords and ladies to pop singers and ordinary Joe Publics. I know this because I've met all these people and they all react in the same way. Ron never ceases to amaze me with the people he has met and the people who have written to him and been to see him over the years. People may knock him but they all want to meet him and they all want to know about him.

Being married to the Colonel has its ups and downs. One of the down-sides is not being able to get an extension on my mortgage because on the application form I have to fill in my husband's occupation, etc. I always get stuck on the occupation question! On the other side, the plus-side, for example, I was stopped by a traffic policeman who, when he saw my name in my driving licence, started to ask me lots of questions. 'No relation to the Kray twins, are you?' he asked. And on it went until he eventually forgot what he had stopped me for. That was good for me – at the time my car had four bald tyres and I had no tax or insurance!

Men, in particular, react dramatically when they learn who I am married to. I remember going with my friend Sharon to a nightclub. There were lots more women than men there but, do you know, every girl in the place was asked to dance except me and Sharon. I felt quite dejected, even though I knew the reason. When I told Ron, he just laughed and said, 'It must have been because you and Sharon were the ugliest ones there!'

Men will often approach me and chat to me, until someone tells them who I am. Then suddenly they will blank me. It's quite funny, really. It's just that name – Kray. Even after all these years people are frightened by it, wary of it, and really there is no need to be.

Marriage to Ron also has its amusing moments. He read in a newspaper about a woman motorist being attacked by a man after her car broke down. This worried him because he knows I spend hours on motorways driving up and down to Broadmoor to see him. So he bought me a portable phone, which was a kind thing to do. Everything was fine until one day I got a message from him in Broadmoor on my portable phone. What's wrong with that? Well, I was standing in the check-out queue at Safeways at the time! There were some very interested ladies in that queue on that particular day, I can tell you. And he only wanted to make sure I was okay. He worries about me.

As I've been putting down on paper my own small part in Ron's story, I've been thinking a lot about my marriage to him. And I still believe, given the chance all over again, I wouldn't change a thing. I intend to stay married to Ron for the rest of my life. What I want more than anything is for him to be released, to be able to come home, to know a real home for the first time since he was just a boy. I truly believe that the only thing keeping both him and Reg inside is their name. It makes ordinary people frightened and I believe it still makes the authorities frightened. Yet I know that the ordinary people of this country believe that both Ron and Reg *should* be freed, I know this because I get letters about it from all over Britain. Almost without exception their theme is the same: enough is enough, the twins have served long enough. They should be freed.

Whenever newspapers have carried out polls among their readers the result has also been the same. For example, the *Sun* carried out a huge poll in 1991 and found a massive vote in favour of the twins' release. Their columnist Gary Bushell wrote about Reg:

> The average sentence for murder is eight years. Many murderers have done their time and built themselves new lives while Kray has languished in chokey . . . For seventeen and a half years he was a Category A prisoner, banged up alone for twenty-three hours a day . . . it is a miracle that he has still got all his marbles.

Contrast that, as Ron does, to the perverted vermin who

killed little Jason Swift . . . The ringleaders got fifteen
years . . . It is unjust to punish Reggie Kray further. He
should be released now. There's as much chance of him
leading a new crime gang as there is of Ted Heath becoming
Prime Minister again.

The headline over the article, while typically *Sun*, really did say
it all: 'It's Kray-zy to keep Reg banged up.'

And I believe the same applies to Ron. I know that his
situation is different because of his medical problems but I also
know, because his doctors at Broadmoor have told me, that Ron
could be released, with safety, provided that he was supervised,
provided that he received the correct medication and provided
that he was properly looked after. Well, he would be looked
after – by me. My husband is not a dangerous maniac. He is a
quiet, gentle man who is no longer a young man. He will soon be
officially an old-age pensioner. Honestly, what sort of gangland
threat would he be now? I appeal to the Home Office seriously
to review the cases of both Ron and Reg. They should be
released, no matter what restrictions accompany that release.
Restrictions they can cope with; being constantly locked away
they can't.

I will continue to campaign for release for both of them for
as long as it takes. I have had to take a lot of stick from
newspapers and magazines because of my beliefs, and because of
who I am married to. Some of the articles written about me have
been actionable, according to my solicitor. But I haven't taken
any action, I haven't attempted to fight back, because that would
mean more mud flying around in the press – and mud sticks. No,
all I want is justice and fairness. Is that too much to ask?

As I've said previously, I would love to be able to have
more contact with Ron. I know there are plans to install
payphones at Broadmoor which the patients would be able to
use at certain times. This will be very welcome and is a much-
needed facility. It is wrong that patients – and they are patients,

as well as prisoners – are not able to talk to their loved ones, particularly at times of stress. I'm sure that when Ron is 'going into one', when he's got one of his bad spells gripping him, I would be able to help the hospital staff, and Ron himself, simply by talking to him over the telephone.

I've read that the Home Officer minister, Angela Rumbold, believes that prisoners should be allowed much more physical contact with their loved ones. She believes, for example, that if prisoners were allowed contact with their wives it would lead to far fewer riots in prisons, fewer suicides and fewer divorces among the country's fifty thousand inmates.

Mrs Rumbold said: 'What happened in Strangeways jail couldn't just be put down to overcrowding and bad conditions. It seems to me that if you are trying to get people to learn lessons from being in prison, it doesn't help if you break up their family and they've absolutely nothing to come out to.'

At the moment, at Broadmoor any show of affection between a patient and his loved one is not welcomed and, in any case, everything there is so public that it is difficult to show affection openly. I think this is sad.

And so life goes on. I send a phone message to my husband every night, I see him as often as they will allow me. I shall go on being Mrs Ronnie Kray, I shall stay faithful to my man and I shall continue to pray that the day will come when we can truly be man and wife.

After all, I married my Ron 'for better or for worse'. And things can only get better. Can't they?

CHAPTER EIGHT

Odds and Sods

O ver the years I've been inside I have met many young cons who told me they couldn't face their sentence, couldn't survive the long years inside. A lot of them have spoken of trying to commit suicide. I have always done my best to talk them out of it. I would never try to commit suicide. I once thought about it, when I was just a young boy, but I would never do so again. Me and Reg have had a pact which we agreed on many years ago. We agreed that we would never give in, we would see our sentences through to the end. No matter how long it takes, no matter how bad it gets, no matter what we have to go through. Me and Reg, we don't see each other much now. We used to meet up about once every three months; they would bring Reg to Broadmoor from whatever prison he was in and we would have a chat for a couple of hours. But it was a long way for him to come, whether he was in Parkhurst or Gartree, and especially now he's in Suffolk, because the screws here would never leave us alone to talk in private. They would always make sure several screws were listening in to our private conversations. So, we were never allowed to talk to each other like we wanted to, like brothers should. So we more or less decided not to worry about the visits. We will just have them, say, a couple of times a year. But we write to each other a lot and pass any urgent messages through various friends who come to see us. We are still very close, after all these years, and despite everything we have gone through.

Whatever we have to face, it will never be as bad as what a young boy called James Fallon had to face. We like to feel we were friends of James, though we never met him. He was only ten but he was paralysed from the neck down after a tragic road accident. He was hit by a car. He couldn't speak, couldn't move. All he could do was signal with his eyes. He was in bed for years like that, before he died. He couldn't do anything other people could do. It was terrible for him. But he always had a smile on his face, right to the end. Me and Reg tried to raise money for him, to make his life more bearable. I still have a photograph of him which I always keep close to me. These days I tell people who are unhappy about little James. We are all a lot better off than he was, we have to count the blessings in life.

People should realize how lucky they are: don't moan, don't take life for granted. People are always moaning about their lives. But James Fallon would have changed places with everyone else, even with me and Reg, just to be able to walk and talk. It's too terrible to think about. That's why I always tell young cons never to give up. I also tell them not to get bitter, not to go around slagging other people off. I show them a few words which an old con once gave to me on a bit of paper: 'There is so much good in the worst of us, so much bad in the best of us, it hardly becomes any of us to talk about the rest of us.'

I wish some other people would listen to those words, too. By that I mean certain people on the outside. People like Leonard 'Nipper' Read, for example.

Read, who claimed the credit for arresting us, was always just another copper in my eyes. I never knew much about him.

But, despite what he did to us, we've always treated him with respect, never slagged him off. But he's not treated us fair. He wrote a book and he had a right go at me and Reg. He said we never showed any remorse and he said we should stay locked up. That was out of order. I'm not complaining about myself, I've done all this time. But how can he say my brother, Reggie, shouldn't get out? As I'm writing this he's done twenty-five years inside. Nipper Read can't have any idea what that is like. He hasn't got a clue what my brother has gone through. He's just being spiteful. He's being a spiteful bastard.

He's not the only one. There's others. We've done nothing to any of them, we've done none of them any harm, yet they've said some terrible things about us. One even said we sent him some dead rats in the post. We never did. We'd known him when we were young boxers, but we never really had any dealings with him. He's got no cause to slag us off.

Tony Lambrianou is nothing but a lackey and a grass. He grassed us when we were all locked up waiting for trial. Nipper Read went to see him when we were on appeal and Lambrianou said to him: 'The Krays done the murders. It was nothing to do with me and my brother.' That's what he said – and so did his brother, Chris. And I can still get the statements to prove it. They both put all the blame on me and Reg, they both said they were innocent. They both grassed us.

Now Tony Lambrianou is outside he's acting like a big gangster. But he never was a big gangster, not even in the old days. He was never a real member of the Firm, he was nothing but an errand boy. He's a ponce, he ponces off our name. He don't care about Reggie trying to get out of prison, trying to get his release. No, he still carries on writing bad stories about us.

I'll tell you what Lambrianou was – he was my errand boy. He used to run around for me. That's all he was good for, Tony Lambrianou, and that's all his brother, Chris, was good for, too. They were nothing to us, nothing to me and Reg. They were nothing on the Firm. But Tony Lambrianou is still living off our name now to make himself money. He even wrote a book about his 'life of crime' with me and Reg, and that was a load of rubbish, too. The only truthful things he said in it were these:

> What the Krays did in London was keep the peace. They kept all the villainy under control. They hated grasses, sex offenders, people who committed crimes to do with women and children. And they couldn't stand petty criminals, like housebreakers.
>
> They'd never have stood for the muggings and the sort of street violence that's going on today.
>
> It was often said the twins could have two hundred armed men on the streets within an hour if they wanted. But they were an army on their own. There will never be another two like them.
>
> They had their own keen sense of values. They would always take the side of the underdog if they thought someone was taking a liberty with a weaker person.
>
> Their loyalty to members of the Firm was absolute and they expected the same loyalty in return. They gave their men a good living and a lifestyle that included all the fringe benefits you could think of.

Tony Lambrianou was right. We hated grasses. We still do. But that's what he was.

And he's right when he says the loyalty we gave to members of our Firm was absolute. We would have died for them, me and Reg. And, yes, we did expect the same loyalty in return. But did we get it? Did we fuck! Only from a few of them, people like Ian Barrie, Freddie Foreman and our brother Charlie. The rest of 'em were like rats deserting a sinking ship. We learned a hard lesson, me and Reg, from the rest of those disloyal bastards. But we knew very early on that a lot of them were giving evidence against us to save their own skins.

What really sticks in my throat is the way some of them are

still trying to make money out of us, and some of them weren't even on the Firm in the first place. They were just 'faces' that we vaguely knew, but they were never anything to us.

There are so many idiots about, all trying to make money out of our name. There was a feller called Dr Glen Wilson, who called himself a top psychiatrist. One of the Sunday paper colour supplements paid him good money to read murderers' minds through their art. He may call himself a top psychiatrist, but I think he's a right idiot. He got a painting by my brother Reg, showing three pyramids in the desert and a moon shining above them. He wrote: 'His work shows a childlike mind lacking in imagination. The pyramids, large and impressive, are probably reflections of how he sees himself.' How can he say Reg is lacking in imagination? He's written five books, some of them without any help from professional writers or journalists; he ran London with me when he was only twenty-four years old, he did. We ran the London underworld together. He's travelled, he's done lots of things, yet this mug says he's got no imagination – and some fancy newspaper has paid him good money for his stupid comments.

They've got hold of one of my paintings as well. It's a painting of a house with a tree next to it. The house is orange with a yellow roof, and everything else is black, except the sky which is purple. They just happened to be the colours I had next to me when I did the painting. This Dr Wilson says: 'Painted by an immature mind, this picture reveals a freedom fantasy and strong desire to be at home.'

Now, I'll tell you and this mug something, and it's the truth: I never, ever worry about getting outside, so I don't know where he gets that from. I've never worried about getting outside, I'm quite happy here at Broadmoor. If I get out, I get out, and that will be great. If I don't, I don't. I don't worry about it. And I wouldn't bow down to someone like Nipper Read to get out. I wouldn't tell a load of lies about feeling sorry, just to get out. I'm not a hypocrite. I know Nipper Read and people like him want to see me and Reg down on our knees, saying how sorry we are for all we've done. But we're not, so why should we be hypocrites and pretend we are, just to please people like that? They can stick their parole where it belongs.

There have been so many accusations against us over the years, most of them just bloody lies. For instance, let's take Freddie Mills. He was the former light heavyweight champion of the world and a very popular man. But he was found shot dead in his car in an alley at the back of a nightclub he owned in the Charing Cross Road. He was shot in the right eye and the coroner's verdict was suicide. Two accusations have been made about us and Freddie Mills. First, his wife, Chrissie, never accepted it was suicide, that Freddie shot himself. She believed he was murdered and that me and Reg killed him. Second, a correspondent wrote in a Sunday newspaper that me and Freddie Mills had been lovers. Both of those things are lies.

Me and Reg knew Freddie Mills a bit when we were kids. He was a big star, then, and he used to train at Ted Broadribb's gym, where we used to go. We used to get the bandages for Freddie's hands, when he was sparring, and we would help him put them on. But we were just kids to him. We never knew him much when we got older. We had a meal once in a Chinese restaurant he owned, but we never went to his club and we never had any business dealings with him. We certainly never killed him or had anything to do with his death. You have my word on that. And I certainly wasn't involved with him in any sexual way. You have my word on that, too.

And I am pleased to say that Nipper Read, of all people, backs us up in his book. He tells how Mrs Mills went to him and claimed Freddie had been killed by someone – and that the killers could have been me and Reg.

Read says in his book he was happy to investigate the death of Freddie Mills. Like us – and like most people in the country – he admired Freddie. Mills was like us: he'd come from nothing. He was an ex-fairground fighter who, in 150 fights, got to the top

of his profession. We admired him like we admired all fighters.
Read says:

> In essence the murder theory ran as follows. The Krays
> had been known to take over clubs. The Krays frequented
> Mills's club. There was money missing from Freddie's
> estate – something like twelve thousand pounds, which was
> big money then. There had been an unsuccessful arson
> attack on his club. There was the story that some weeks
> before Freddie's death small club owners who were a bit
> lax in paying protection were told something big was going
> to happen, and this would be an example to them. Freddie
> had obtained a gun to protect himself, and he left the club
> saying he was going to an appointment.

Read says he spoke to members of our Firm, who told him,
'No way. When the twins went to Freddie's place they paid,
they'd never nip him. They were boxers, too. He was their hero.'
He also managed to establish that Freddie's club was never on
our protection list.

Leonard Read agreed with the verdict of the coroner. He
wrote: 'I have to look at it on the evidence and, based on that, I
am sadly forced to the inescapable conclusion that he did, in fact,
take his own life.' And that's the truth of it. We never did
Freddie Mills in. And, even though I have admitted I am
bisexual, there was never anything going on between me and
Freddie. And I want that to be the end of it.

Funnily enough, it was a student, a young girl called Susan
Gilchrist, who seemed to understand the harm that has been
done to me and Reg, particularly to him because he should be
out by now. And would be were it not for others. In March 1991,
Ms Gilchrist wrote a dissertation for Newcastle upon Tyne
Polytechnic called: 'The Kray Twins: Some observations on the
power of sub-culture and aspects of tabloid journalism'. I think
it is fair to say that, by the end of her research, Ms Gilchrist –

whom I have never met – was very disturbed at the way Reg and I have been treated by many newspapers, many journalists and some writers. And she believes their words have added to our misery. She says: 'The lack of serious interest in the Krays is disturbing. Irresponsible journalists take them both further and further away from freedom. A closer look at the Kray twins reveals very different men from those "leading thugs of the underworld" who regularly appear menacingly from the pages of the tabloid newspapers.'

That, I think, says it all. I hope, for my brother's sake, someone will listen. Honestly, he's not the bad man many people make him out to be. Ask a little lad from Nottingham called Paul Stapleton who suffers from multiple sclerosis. It was Reg's fund-raising that sent that little boy to Disneyland in America. Ask the many other children and adults he's raised money for. A lot of people say he shouldn't be let out, but they are wrong. Reg has paid his dues. It's time now for a little compassion. For us both.

CHAPTER NINE

Broadmoor Legends

Legend Unreliable story, based on oral tradition but popularly thought to have some factual basis.
Penguin English Dictionary

Every business has its characters, its special people. Sport does, so does show business. And so does Broadmoor. Here in Broadmoor there have been some special people, fellers who stand out from the crowd. Some of them are famous, others will have been heard of by no one outside the walls of the hospital. But they are all what I call the Broadmoor Legends.

In sort of alphabetical order, they are . . .

A – for the Axeman. Frank Mitchell, the so-called Mad Axeman. One of the biggest, strongest and yet gentlest men I've ever met. Six foot two, eighteen stone, Frank is one of the greatest of the Broadmoor Legends, because there has never been anyone quite like him. No prison or mental hospital could ever hold him if he didn't want to stay there. Frank could escape from anywhere. He could do press-ups till the cows came home, often using only one hand, and he could carry a full-size billiard table on his back. Yet he was also a gentle man who used to make beautiful wooden toys for children.

Frank wasn't mad. The papers just called him the Mad Axeman because once, when he was on the run, he threatened someone with an axe. He had a good sense of humour. He once tied a towel round a nurse's neck and made out that he was going to throttle him. The nurse was in a blind panic, and all he could think of to say, was: 'Leave off, Frank. Tomorrow's me day off!' Frank laughed – and let him go. They said we killed Frank Mitchell, but we never did. He was one of our best friends.

B – for Birnnie, Bob. Known as the Joker because he is always telling jokes. He makes people laugh, even in Broadmoor. He is a very good friend of mine. Bob was in the 1979 riot at the Scrubs (Wormwood Scrubs) where the screws split his head open with batons. Bob has always been a rebel but is a nice man who has always been respected in prison and Broadmoor.

B – for the Bed-spring Swallower. A very famous con when he was at Parkhurst, and Reg knew him when he was there. He was eventually certified and sent to Broadmoor. I never knew his proper name, he was just known as the Bed-spring Swallower. This was because he was always swallowing the springs from his bed! The doctors were always having to cut him open to get them out.

Reg tells the story of how this feller once got upset with his brother, who was on the outside. His brother had a beautiful garden, which was his pride and joy. So, to get his own back on his brother, the Bed-spring Swallower – who was in for murder, by the way – contacted the police and told them he had buried a body in his brother's garden. It wasn't true, of course, but the police had to check it out – and that meant digging up the entire plot! The brother was upset by this, but when the Bed-spring Swallower heard the news of the ruined garden he was pleased and he decided that all policemen were wonderful fellers!

C – for Costello, Jimmy. Although he's only five feet four inches tall, Jimmy is a tough little feller from Glasgow, who made headlines when he attacked Peter Sutcliffe, the Yorkshire Ripper, when they were both in Parkhurst prison. Jimmy cut him with a piece of glass from a broken coffee jar, and the wound needed eighty-four stitches. That was in 1983 and in a newspaper article in 1991, Jimmy wrote that it had made him a public hero overnight. He said: 'I even got fan mail from America and Australia. But it also cost me the love of my fiancée, Rae, the love of my life, because I got extra time for attacking Sutcliffe and she said she couldn't face waiting for me any longer.' In the same newspaper article Jimmy wrote: 'Groups like MIND and Mencap helped me inside, but the only other people who helped me were Reg and Ron Kray. They were good friends to me.'

Jimmy is now a free man and looking after his little son, Jamie. He also tries to raise money for the mental health groups who helped him when he was inside.

C – for Clark, Nobby. Not a well-known name on the outside, but another London feller who's done his time in Broadmoor. He's been a good friend to me, he's shown loyalty and gameness. These are things which have always been important to me.

D – for the Doctor. A pleasant feller who was in Broadmoor, who used to call himself Dr Swan. He wasn't really a qualified doctor, but he had such an amazing knowledge of medical matters he even used to tell the doctors here what to do. It's said that sometimes they even took his advice! A lot of the patients here are articulate and intelligent, despite what people on the outside might think. They are not savages, they are personalities in their own right.

E – for Ernie. That's how he was known. He did twenty-two years in Broadmoor and he's now out. He was a good friend. When a young screw kept on having a go at him, Ernie said to the flash bastard: 'If you keep on having a go at me I will get a bucket of scalding water and pour it over you.' Ernie was a man of his word and would have done so. The screw knew this and got shifted to another ward.

F – for Fraser, Frank. Better known as Mad Frankie. I never thought he was mad, not even when he was giving us a few problems when he was with the Richardson gang, south of the river. One of the most feared villains in London, Frank is a very powerfully built man who was admired because of his gameness. He is a good friend of ours and has been to see me in Broadmoor. He is one of the old school and would not grass on anyone. He was recently shot in the face, but survived, and when the police asked him who did it, he said, 'Tutankhamun' . . . and wouldn't give any more information. Frank has spent more than half his life in prison and has attacked more screws than anyone else in the history of prisons. He did three years in Broadmoor and was then freed. To show there was never personal animosity between the Krays and Mad Frankie, Frank offered to give evidence for us during our trial. We appreciated that.

F – for Fryer, Mad Ronnie. A good friend of mine here, when he was released from Broadmoor he had a row with his best friend and knifed him to death. He was charged with murder and sent to Brixton prison on remand, where sadly he committed suicide. He's still spoken of well at Broadmoor.

G – for Gibbons, Julie and Jennifer. Known as the Silent Twins. They are in the female block at Broadmoor. Two attractive girls who were sent here for arson. When they came here they spoke to no one except each other for two years, and no one could understand what they said to each other. Nowadays they do talk to some other people.

H – for Hume, Donald. Like others here, Donald was found guilty of murder. He got a lot of publicity in the fifties after he murdered a man in Germany. He was sent to prison there and he had a tough time. After many appeals, the Germans finally agreed to him being sent to Broadmoor. I remember him saying to me once: 'Compared to prison in Germany, this place is like Buckingham Palace.'

J – for Joseph, Father Joseph, as he is known here. A lovely old character. He's not really a priest, but he goes around giving everyone his blessing. He used to be a violent man but now he is very religious. He prays a lot and he listens to the problems of some of the patients here and tries to help them in his own way. He does more good than most of the padres and so-called men of God I've ever met inside.

K – for Knight, 'Bogie'. An ex-Chindit who won medals for bravery in the war. He was tortured by the Japanese and it turned his mind. He became violent and they sent him here. He's always been well liked. He's an old man now and in the infirmary at Broadmoor. But the nurses treat him well. They respect him. They know he was a brave man who did his duty. If it hadn't been for those Jap bastards he would probably have been okay.

L – for Lingford Gardiner. One of the strongest men I have ever met. He is black; a giant of a man who became a Broadmoor legend because of his power. I once saw him lift a chair with a feller called Gus sitting on it. And Gus weighed sixteen stone!

They say that when Lingford was arrested before they brought him here four policemen broke their truncheons on his head. I don't know what his crime was, patients in Broadmoor don't often discuss with each other what their crimes have been, but I do know that he was a good friend of mine for the ten years he was here. When my mother died he went to her funeral. How he found his way to Chingford cemetery I do not know, because he could not read or write. Yet when I arrived at the cemetery on that day in August 1982, in all the fuss and commotion I heard someone call out my name. I turned, and it was Lingford. That day was the last time I left the hospital until ten years later, in 1992, when I had an operation at a local hospital. It was also the last time I saw this particular Broadmoor legend.

O – for Oberdine. The only name he was known by. A black feller, short and thick-set and built like a tank. He was terribly strong. When the police first arrested him he was in a flat in Notting Hill Gate, in London. It was only a minor charge but they knew he was a danger, so they sent a police Alsatian dog into the flat first. Oberdine got hold of the dog – and bit its throat out. The police overpowered him eventually and he was sent to Dartmoor prison. While in prison he was stabbed in the back by another con during a service in the chapel. Oberdine pulled the knife out of his back – and slashed five other cons with it. He was then sent to Broadmoor where the screws were very wary of him and did not bother him much. Finally, after three years here, he was released. He went back to West Africa, where he came from, and was later shot dead by the police.

P – for Peterson, Mick, alias Charles Bronson. I was in Parkhurst prison with him and I saw him split open a screw's eye with a punch. He then came to Broadmoor where he climbed up on the roof of Somerset House, smashed it up, and caused a million pounds' worth of damage. All of the patients in the block had to be moved while the damage was repaired. Another time he picked up the governor on his shoulders and carried him to his room, where he held him hostage. Finally, they moved him back to prison and the last I heard of him some cons had done him with a knife. But Mick refused to name the men who had done him. He was always a man with a lot of principles. But Mick, like a lot of patients and prisoners, does need help. My brother remembers a time when he was walking with him at Parkhurst, just chatting, when he noticed Mick go white around his nostrils. Mick then walked away, marched straight up to a toilet door and butted the windows in. He then sat down as though greatly relieved. His moment of madness had passed. But of such moments legends are made.

R – for Reeves, Alan. A good friend and one of the lucky ones who got away from Broadmoor. But, like a lot of patients, the Broadmoor curse seemed to follow him. Later he killed a policeman in Holland and he was in prison there.

R – for Roza, Jack. Another one who got out of Broadmoor but never escaped the curse of the place. We knew Jack and his brother Ray who used to be a minder for Billy Hill. Jack was serving a sentence in Wandsworth, where a screw kept on having a go at him. Jack was game and would not stand for this, so he stole a thick needle from the mail bag shop where he worked. He then waited by the spyhole in his cell door, knowing that the screw would come along to check on him. Jack waited till the screw put his eye up to the spyhole – and then stabbed him right in the eye. The screw was blinded, and Jack was sent to Broadmoor. He was here three years before they let him out, but shortly after he was in a car crash. Even then he showed his bravery by crawling away from the wreckage for four miles to get help. But he finally died. A nice man and a friend of ours.

S – for Shaw, Roy. He did three years in Broadmoor. He is a very strong, powerful fighter. While he was here he had a fight with a feller called Freddie Mills – no relation to the boxer – who, like Roy, was a very game man. The fight lasted an hour and a half before the screws broke it up. They were both badly cut and bleeding, but ended up good friends. While he was here Roy broke a screw's jaw. After he was released he came back to Broadmoor to visit me a few times. A good friend.

S – for Silvers, John. Another giant – six feet eight inches tall – and very, very strong. I first met him when I was on remand in Brixton and he was in for murder. For a while we were on the same ward at Broadmoor and I found him good company. He spent fourteen years in the punishment block, something of a record, because he kept punching screws on the chin. It was like a sport to him and he was later transferred to Park Lane hospital, to see if that would help. It is doubtful that it did.

S – Smith, Charlie. Fearless Charlie Smith they call him, and he is. My best friend in Broadmoor who, with luck, will be out by the time you read this. A great musician who has released a cassette of his own songs, all recorded inside his room in the hospital on his own simple recorder, and he's raised a lot of money for charity. He's a fighter, is Charlie, a fighter for justice. He even took the authorities to the High Court in a bid to make them release details of the whereabouts of his mother. He lost the case, but it shows the determination of the little feller. The friendship of Charlie is one of the best things that has happened in my years at Broadmoor.

S – for Smithers, Mike. One of the bravest men in Broadmoor. An ex-boxer who attacked a screw in the punishment block – a place where the screws are God – and tried to bite his ear off.

S – Sutcliffe, Peter. The so-called Yorkshire Ripper who will become a Broadmoor legend, sadly, because of his terrible crimes against women. I bear him no malice because he is a sick man. But I could never condone what he did; I could never accept him as a friend. In fact, we laugh at him. One morning a screw opened the door to his room and shouted out, 'Hallo, Jack!' You have to have a sense of humour here, though I don't think Sutcliffe found that very funny.

T – is for Trevor. That's the only name he's known by. Tall and slim with big, long, bony hands. He once strangled a man to death with his bare hands. He now takes care of the sick patients. No one is without a cigarette when Trevor is around. He has been with me for fifteen years and every week he gives my neck a massage. I can feel the strength in his hands, but somehow I know that he won't try and hurt me. He is a kind and caring man! We all know him as Gentleman Trevor.

W – Watt, Joe. Another black feller, famous here for his size and amazing strength. In the end Joe got so big and so heavy that Charlie Smith said to him one day: 'You better lose some weight, Joe, otherwise it will kill you.' Within days, Joe was dead of a heart attack. Yet another Broadmoor legend who never made it back to the world outside.

So these are just some of the men and women whose names will live on in this place long after they, and I, have passed on. To them and all of the patients in this hospital I have a simple message:

I pray for you at night
That God will always give you light,
And when you are meek he will give you might.

When each day comes around,
He will help you through each day's struggle and fight,
I'm your friend and will always do for you what is right,
To me you are higher than a bird in flight.

All you may not see and may not hear
But never doubt and never fear,
As I am your friend and will always be here.

When they've all passed you by,
I will stand by your side,
And when I said I was your friend I never lied;
I say this with pride,
As God is my judge and God is my guide.

CHAPTER TEN

Seeing Stars

R eg and I have been seeing stars for years. Right from the days when we were young villains on the streets of the East End we always seem to have attracted the company of show-business and sporting people. Sportsmen, of course, we've admired since we were little kids – especially boxers – but we've usually got along well with show people, as we call them. Mind you, you have to watch out for some of them. They can be a bit unstable. I remember, back in the sixties, a world-famous pop star came to see me and Reg and asked us if we could let him have a gun. We asked him what for and he told us he and another feller had had a row over some woman – and he wanted to shoot the other bloke! No way were me and Reg going to do time for a nutcase like that, even if he was a nice feller, and even if he was top of the charts. So we politely told him to fuck off.

But I'm pleased to say that a lot of our famous friends, those that are still fit and alive, have carried on visiting me and Reg even after we were put away. They weren't just fairweather friends who just wanted to know us during the good times.

The first famous person me and Reg ever met was a Jewish boxer from the East End called Young Ashell Joseph. He was welterweight champion of Great Britain in the twenties. Our father took us to meet him near Petticoat Lane, in London. When we met him he was in a wheelchair, paralysed from the waist down. We gave him a small picture we had of him when he was a boxer. It was like a cigarette card. When we gave him the picture of himself his face lit up. I will never forget his smile, because when he smiled he had all gold teeth. He was the first famous person we ever met, and we were proud to do so.

One of the first real stars we got to know was Winifred Atwell, a black honky-tonk piano player, sadly now dead, who had huge hits in the fifties with records like 'Poor People of Paris'. I first met her at the Green Gate pub, in Bethnal Green. We had a drink or two together and got on like a house on fire. Later she used to visit the Kentucky club, which we owned, and sometimes we would go to her house. Winnie helped me and Reg raise a lot of money for boys' clubs in the East End and, funnily enough, she put on a concert for the patients at Broadmoor, which I arranged many years before I came here. I still have one of her albums, signed with a personal message.

We've known many other show-business stars, like Roger Daltrey, lead singer with the Who. Roger is nothing like his 'wild man' image and is a very deep, thoughtful feller. He gave my friend Charlie Smith a guitar the Who had used on one of their American tours. He's a fair actor, too, and he played the part of John McVicar, in the film *McVicar*. I would say that Roger is far more of a man and much less of a poseur than McVicar, though. McVicar is a one-time small-time villain who now makes his living writing and talking about real villains.

Diana Dors was one of our favourite show-business people, a great actress and a very special person. Reggie first spotted her singing at the Room at the Top, at Ilford, and he came home raving about 'this fantastic girl with platinum blonde hair'. We got very close with Diana and her husband, Alan Lake, and

Diana used to visit me, Reg and Charlie inside. She also used to go round and visit our parents at their home in Vallance Road. She always took them gifts of fruit and flowers and my mother thought the sun shone out of her. Alan used to come and see me and Reg in Parkhurst. The first time he came to see us they wouldn't let him in because they said he had a criminal record. He didn't make a fuss about it, he just went home and started writing letters to the authorities until they would let him visit us. Once Diana died, though, that was the beginning of the end for Alan. We watched him go downhill and there was nothing anyone could do about it. He had loved her so much, and he just lost the will to live.

We thought the great American entertainer Billy Daniels had lost the will to live, once, but for a very different reason. Billy was famous for a song called 'That Old Black Magic'. We used to go clubbing a lot with him and he was a nice feller, though he sometimes liked the drink a bit too much. Once, in the sixties, Reggie saved him from getting a good hiding. Billy had been having a few drinks at a hotel in London with Reg and some other fellers, when Billy got a bit heavy with Tommy Brown, an ex-boxer who used to be called the Bear. Tommy got a bit fed up and he would have flattened Billy if Reg hadn't stopped him. The next night Billy missed a performance at the London Palladium to come round to the Kentucky club to apologize to Tommy, and to give Reg a pair of gold cuff-links as a gesture of goodwill. It's not the only time Billy nearly got himself in very serious bother. It's said that he once upset a New York Mafia boss named Crazy Joe Gallo, by taking out an air hostess who was one of Joe's girlfriends. Billy was picked up by some of Gallo's men and taken to a basement where Crazy Joe used to keep a caged lion. It was said he would let the lion attack anyone who upset him. Billy got on his knees and apologized to Joe, who let him off with a warning. Billy laughed about it afterwards. He used to say: 'I never felt the same way about air hostesses, or lions, after that!'

David Essex was another singer we knew and liked. In fact me and Reg gave him his first singing break in our club the El Morocco, in Gerrard Street, Soho. We called it that because it reminded us of some happy times we had in Morocco. David was one of the first entertainers we signed up to do a regular spot. He was a complete unknown then. He's never forgotten us and on a Christmas television show, a few years back, he sent his best wishes to me and Reg and Charlie.

The actor Ronald Fraser was an early show-business friend. We'd see him often at race meetings and he used to come to all our clubs, especially the Kentucky, the Double R, and the Cambridge Rooms. Ronnie was a good actor who knew how to enjoy himself. I'll never forget when me and Reg once bought a horse called Solway Cross for our mum. We had it trained at Epsom, but we thought we'd bought a bummer when it came last in its first race. So we decided to raffle it one night at the Cambridge Rooms, to make some money for charity. Ronnie won the raffle but he was so pissed I don't think he realized it. He woke up next morning with a racehorse he hadn't got a clue what to do with!

Debbie Harry, who had five number one records in the late seventies, has been to see me at Broadmoor, Marvin Gaye wrote to me pledging his support for me and Reg, and, of course, we were close friends of one of the greatest entertainers of all time, Judy Garland.

Judy became a friend when she used to come to our clubs. She would always come to see us when she was in London, and we would always have the best seats for her shows, and go backstage afterwards. Often our mother would come with us because she was a big fan of Judy's. Judy sent a telegram when Reg married Frances, and I made headlines during our trial when I told the judge: 'If I wasn't here now, I'd probably be having a gin and tonic with Judy Garland.' The funny thing was, I probably would have, because Judy was in London at the time. I once met Dirk Bogarde, with Judy Garland, and he seemed a right nice man.

Charlton Heston, the American actor, was another one who came to our trial and he later sent me a letter. Jon Bon Jovi, the American rock singer, is another who writes and sends me cards. He has promised he will come and see me in Broadmoor when he is next in Britain. The Kemp twins, Gary and Martin, who used to be in Spandau Ballet, have been to see me and Reg, because they played us in the film *The Krays*. I think they do look a lot like us when we were young.

Helen Keating, the actress, grew up with us in the East End. We have known each other since we were kids and have had a lifelong friendship. She is a star now in programmes like *London's Burning*. But she still stays in touch with us.

The singer Kenny Lynch has stayed loyal, and we've known him since he joined in the boxing bouts we used to stage when we were kids in our house in Vallance Road. It was tough on him being a black kid in the East End all those years ago, but Kenny always stood up for himself well. The actors Glen Murphy and Billy Murray have stayed loyal, too. I remember, in the early days, Billy was having trouble getting an Equity card and, unless you belong to the actors' union you can't get work as an actor. Billy explained his problem to us and we sent him to Billy Hill who, at the time, ran a lot of London's underworld. It was said at the time that Billy could fix anything and we always thought he was the ultimate professional criminal. Shortly after seeing Hill, Billy Murray got his Equity card. Like I said, we spotted David Essex early in his career, and Eric Clapton made one of his earliest professional appearances at our club Esmerelda's Barn. That was thanks to a feller called Laurie O'Leary, who managed the club for us. Laurie's brother, Alfie, ended up taking a job with Eric Clapton and he travelled all over the world with him. The Walker Brothers, whose record was playing on the juke box the night I shot George Cornell, also played at the Barn. Laurie O'Leary later went on to become a real entrepreneur and he's stayed a mate of ours for many years.

So did the blind singer Lenny Peters until his sad death in

1992. Lenny found fame when he teamed up with a girl called Diane Lee and they became known as Peters and Lee. When he was first starting out he came and saw me and I got him a booking at the Blue Angel club in the West End. He also worked at several of our clubs. He never forgot the helping hand and he came to Broadmoor several times to put on shows for the patients. He was an amazing feller. Even though he was blind he would always know instantly whenever Reg or I walked into a room. I'll always remember a big charity do we put on at the Cambridge Rooms. Lenny was doing the cabaret and the guest of honour was Sonny Liston, the former heavyweight boxing champion of the world. It was almost impossible to make Liston laugh and he was known as Old Stoneface. Yet, as he listened to a special song Lenny had written about him, called Old Stoneface, Liston just broke up with laughter. It was a magic moment.

Joe Pyle was another friend from the early days who became a great entrepreneur. When we first met him at the Double R he was a promising middleweight boxer, but his career was ruined when he was arrested for the shooting of a man called Cooney in the Pen club, near Spitalfields Market. He went on trial at the Old Bailey but was eventually acquitted. These days he runs a film production company and manages singers. He's visited me consistently over the years at Broadmoor and brought many famous celebrities with him. The last time me and Reg were outside we had a drink with Joe at the Astor club, to celebrate the birth of his son. These days Joe junior, as well as Joe senior, comes to see me.

The great American actor George Raft was another close friend. Me and Reggie first met him in the Colony club, in Berkeley Square. At that time he was about seventy-two and I have never seen a more smartly dressed man. He told me he used to have one meal a day, a steak with salad every evening. He was a lovely feller, nothing like his tough-guy image. He used to love looking round the East End, which he said was like New York. I found that to be true when I went there myself. We took our mother and father out with him several times and he gave me and Reg a beautiful gold cigarette lighter each. When I was a kid, watching his films, I never dreamed this great man would one day be my friend.

The English actor Andrew Ray has been a good friend over the years, and he once sent my mother the biggest food and drinks hamper I've ever seen in my life. Another Ray, the American singer, Johnny, was a pal. He made a record called 'Cry' in the fifties which was a number one all over the world. I first met him in the Dolce Vita nightclub in Newcastle. I once gave him a silver bracelet – and he once asked me to loan him ten grand for four weeks. That's the equivalent of nearly a hundred thousand pounds these days. But he was as good as his word and, four weeks later, he returned the money. He once told me he was at his happiest when he was on a stage, singing. Off-stage he didn't have much personality, but on-stage he was full of it.

A singer with personality on-stage and off was Lita Rosa, and she was a very good friend. I'll always remember seeing her perform for the first time. It was at the Royal Ballroom, in Tottenham, and me and Reg were AWOL from the Army at the time. We'd popped into the Royal for a drink, and to hear Lita singing with the Ray Ellington Band. Unfortunately some of the Tottenham lads picked a fight with us and it all ended up in a right old scrap on the dance floor with Lita still singing away as if nothing was happening! Years later, when we were friends, we had a good laugh about that night. And, by the way, me and Reg won the scrap.

George Sewell often plays tough-guy roles in plays and films but, though he looks a hard man, he's very gentle and very good company. He's been a friend for years and has been to see me in Broadmoor, as has another actor, Victor Spinetti.

Sophie Tucker was one of the most interesting friends I ever had. She was a great film star in the twenties, thirties and forties. She was Jewish-American and she once told me Al Capone gave her her start in show-business in one of his speakeasies. She told me he once bought her a necklace for twenty thousand dollars – that's got to be near on two hundred grand these days – and that he was very kind to her. When I asked her what Capone was like, she said: 'He's a nice man – if he likes you.' She would ring me from all over the world, just for a chat, and every time she did I would play her a record of her singing a song called 'My Yiddisher Mama'. It was my favourite song and I still like it. She died when I was in prison and I was sad.

But all our friends aren't just old-timers. The rock band UB40 have been very supportive in recent years. But, of course, one of our very best friends has always been the actress Barbara Windsor. She and her ex-husband Ronnie Knight sent flowers to our mother's funeral, and all the time we've been away Barbara has campaigned harder than anyone to get freedom for Reg. We go back a long way. Early in 1963, a few months after we'd opened the Kentucky club, Barbara asked us if we'd let the club be used in some scenes in a film she was making called *Sparrows Can't Sing*. Her co-stars were Queenie Watts and James Booth. At the end of the year the film's première was held in Stepney and afterwards we had a fantastic party at the Kentucky. Me and Reg bought most of the tickets at the première and made a lot of money for charity. Those were great days. And while I'm talking of show people, I must just mention Norman Wisdom, who's written me some of the funniest letters I've ever received in Broadmoor.

We've had friends from all sorts of backgrounds. Francis Bacon, a great artist, used to gamble at Esmerelda's Barn – *chemin de fer* was his passion. We became very close friends. We met in Tangiers, on holiday, and discovered we had a lot in common – a love of North Africa, art and gambling. Over the years I sent him several of my own paintings so that I could get his comments on them. He has written me many lovely letters and sent me some beautiful cards at Christmas.

David Bailey, the society and fashion photographer, has

also been a close friend. David has settled down now, but he was a real 'Jack the Lad' when he was younger. I remember Reg once asked him what his hobby was. David replied: 'Sex!'

Terry Dene is now a born-again Christian, but in the fifties he was a pop idol and a good friend. He often used to stay at the flat I had in Cedra Court. But, like all show people, Terry used to keep erratic hours. One morning he arrived home in the early hours, pissed. He'd lost his key, so he began climbing up the drainpipe to my bedroom on the second floor. The caretaker saw him, thought he was a burglar, and called the police! These days Terry Dene is a very different sort of man.

But, of course, sportsmen have always been the biggest idols for me and Reg, and some of them have been among our best friends. In the main they've been boxers. Alphabetically speaking, I'm talking of men like . . .

Frank Bruno, who came to see the patients here, and spoke to us and gave away some photographs. He is a gentle man. In his book, he wrote that he could not believe a mild-mannered man like me once ran the London underworld.

David Charnley, the former British and European lightweight champion and the most successful British lightweight for the decade from 1954 to 1964. Boxers are usually straightforward and honest because, as far as the fighters are concerned, it's a straightforward and honest sport. Once you get in that ring it's just you and the other bloke. May the better man win. Dave is a typical boxer in that respect. He's been a good friend, though I still can't explain how a feller from Dartford in Kent talks with a Scottish accent.

John Conteh, ex-middleweight champion of the world, is another good guy who's had to overcome a lot of personal problems. But he's done it like the man he is. John has also got the best set of teeth I've ever seen on a man. How he's managed to keep them after some of the scraps he's been in, God only knows.

Terry Downes, another great British boxer who beat Sugar

Ray Robinson to win a world crown, is one of my boxing favourites. A very tough man, but with a heart of gold. Terry pays regular visits, also, to my friend in Broadmoor, Charlie Smith. He's such a down-to-earth, modest feller, Terry would never realize just how much his visits mean.

Karl Gizzi and *John Griffiths* are two Welsh fighters who come and see me, and John always comes loaded down with books, usually biographies, which he knows I like to read.

Joe Louis, 'The Brown Bomber', was a man whose friendship I valued greatly. Everyone knows that he was one of the greatest fighters of all time and he was in touch with me right up until his death in 1981. In the sixties he used to come to our clubs in the East End and he helped us raise a lot of money for boys' clubs in the area. I once took him to Broadmoor, many years before I was a patient here, to give a talk to some of the patients. I remember him telling the patients about his climb to fame, and how his trainer told him before his first world championship fight: 'I've done all I can for you, Joe. Now it's up to you.' And Joe told the patients: 'The staff here at Broadmoor are doing all they can for you. Now it's up to you.' It was good advice, which I've always remembered. He died in Las Vegas in 1981 after two strokes. The boxing writer Reg Gutteridge once said: 'He was a marvellous heavyweight champion, a decent man. The sport of boxing never produced a more loved person.' I agree with that. Like us, Joe Louis came from a poor background, in his case a dirt farmer's shack in Alabama, but he made it to the very top. I was proud to call him a friend.

Charlie Magri, the ex-flyweight champion of the world is a good friend of ours.

Danny McAllinden, a former British heavyweight champion, and *Pat McAteer*, ex-middleweight champion, have also been good friends. So has *Sammy Reason*, the former British lightweight champion.

And *Terry Spinks*, the former British featherweight champion. Always a good friend and a game little fighter, Terry managed to spend his money quicker than he earned it, but he never lacked friends. A genuine feller. Like *John H. Stracey*, the former world welterweight champion, and another Bethnal Green boy who battled his way out of the slums.

Jimmy Wild was one of the greatest boxers I have ever met. He was flyweight champion of the world. Me and Reggie met him in an old people's home just outside of Cardiff. He was so good they used to call him 'the Ghost with the Hammer in his Hands'. They also used to call him 'The Mighty Atom'. He was one of the greatest fighters who ever lived, and we were very proud to have met him. Poor Jim died in that old people's home.

Among our other sporting friends have been footballers Colin Pates and Justin Fashanu. I was pleased when Justin wrote and told me he wanted to visit me in Broadmoor. He spent much of the time telling me how he'd become a born-again Christian. I think he was hoping to convert me, but I told him: 'I don't need to be reborn to have good thoughts and to look after other people.' Maybe it wasn't what he wanted to hear, but it hasn't stopped us being friends.

The great snooker player Jimmy White has also been to visit me. Even though I am not a snooker follower, I admire his talent and his attitude. He does a lot of good work for charity.

Reg and I have been lucky to know so many good people from show-business and sport, and there are others who have come to see us and written to us. One of the most unusual letters came from the entertainer Max Bygraves. Max wrote to me from Australia a couple of winters ago. He told me he'd been having a quiet drink in a bar in Sydney, when a feller sidled up alongside him and said I was upset at a remark Max had made about the Kray twins in his autobiography. Max said he 'didn't want to kick a man when he was down', and said he would get the offending words taken out of the book. To this day I do not know what he wrote because I have never read his book. But to show there were no hard feelings I sent him a nice ornamental teapot for his wife. When he wrote and thanked me for it, he said: 'I was frightened to open the box at first, Ron. I thought it might be a bomb!'

Reg and I know we have many other friends out there, ordinary people, not famous, but still important to us. Maybe you are one of them. We have had many thousands of letters from ordinary people, too many to answer. But I would like everyone who has written to us to know that we appreciate their thoughts. We have had a lot of support. Twenty-nine thousand people phoned the *Sun* newspaper in June 1989, to say 'Free Reggie Kray'. The paper had asked its readers if they thought it was time to set Reg free, and twenty-nine thousand said yes. At the same time Reg received more than three thousand letters of support and I received nearly one thousand five hundred. That kind of support gives us the strength to carry on, even though sometimes the fight looks hopeless.

Friends have always been very important to me and Reg. He once wrote a poem called 'Friendship' . . . and to me it says it all.

> Friendship is
> An eternity . . . of sorts.
> Valueless, unlike money,
> A true friendship never aborts . . .
> his friend.
> Friendship is
> Stronger than steel,
> Steel will break in the end,
> But what better bond
> Than a true friend?
> Friendship is
> Entirely, utterly selfless,
> Helps you straighten out
> When you are in a mess.
> What more to say?
> Friendship isn't words, it's feeling,

Sharing, caring,
Understanding and believing!
Friendship's qualities
I can't define,
But I have a friend called Ron
Who's a true friend of mine,
And if you look closely,
Ever so closely at Ron,
You'll see diamonds and gold
Are as none,
When compared to the friendship
I share . . . with Ron.

Epilogue

I'm sixty years old now. I've been locked up for twenty-five years. That's what people don't remember, they forget we've been away for so long. People still think we're young, like the photographs show us, like the film about us. But we're not young, not any more. Me and Reg, we're old men, now.

When we were about thirty-five, we used to weigh twelve and a half stone. We were rock solid and my neck used to measure seventeen inches. It doesn't any more, and these days I weigh under eleven stone. These days I'm really skin and bone.

But I'm still not frightened of anyone or anything. I've never been frightened, not once in my life. I'm older now, of course, older and wiser. But I'd do it all again. I wouldn't change anything, because your life is mapped out for you anyway, isn't it? But if I had a son I would tell him not to go into crime. It's a bad thing to go into. Kids should go into sport, boxing, football, running. They can make money at it and it's good for them. Sport is a good thing, crime is no good. I can never escape from my notoriety as a criminal. I hit the headlines yet again in June

1993. The *Star* devoted most its front page to a story headlined 'Ronnie Kray Chokes Nutter'. Their story said: 'Gangland killer Ronnie Kray has tried to strangle another Broadmoor inmate. The victim was seconds away from being throttled to death when staff prised Kray's hands from round this throat.'

The facts are these. The doctors at Broadmoor were bringing my medication level down. They were trying to see if I could do without my drugs. This was a difficult time for me as my body tried to adjust. I was depressed, the weather was hot, the atmosphere was oppressive. I was doing all right, but a patient called Lee Kiernender kept trying to wind me up. Everyone here regards him as a pest. Normally, I would just have told him to fuck off. Unfortunately, with all my problems, when he kept trying to gee me up, I just snapped. I went for him. I didn't really hurt him, but I could have. I think he will stay away from me in future.

The authorities at Broadmoor didn't punish me because they knew they were partly to blame for the problem. My life still goes on as normal. My medication is down a bit, which is a good sign. But the publicity I had over that incident will almost certainly count against me in the future. I don't worry too much about that. I hope it won't affect Reg, though, because this had nothing to do with him.

It's just another chapter in my story, I suppose. It was the first bit of trouble I have had for a long time, it wasn't a major incident, but it still got splashed all over some of the newspapers. It's just part of the price I know I have to pay.

I don't think about the future any more. It's too late for most things now. My life is here, now. This is my life. It's all there is, it's all there probably ever will be. I really don't care any more.

Appendix

Broadmoor's Story

On 15 May 1800, a man called James Hadfield tried to shoot King George III as the King sat in the Royal Box at the Drury Lane Theatre, in the West End of London, watching a play. The theatre was packed with people, many of them there just hoping to catch a glimpse of the King.

At the end of the production the audience cheered the actors and then remained on their feet to cheer King George. He stood up in his box to acknowledge their applause – and that was the moment when Hadfield seized his chance and fired the shot.

Hadfield was unlucky because, at the precise moment when he fired his pistol, the King happened to bow his head to the audience. The bullet narrowly missed him and embedded itself in the theatre wall. The would-be assassin never got another shot in because, as the King slumped back in his seat in a state of shock, members of the audience threw themselves on Hadfield. He was overpowered, the police rushed across and arrested him, and he was carried away shouting. It must have given the King a hell of a fright, though, because later he became mentally ill.

Some weeks later Hadfield came up for trial, charged with high treason, but the case wasn't as open and shut as it might at first have appeared. Hadfield had an interesting defence: he had, he said, been acting on the specific instructions of God, whose voice he had heard quite clearly telling him he had been chosen to save the world, but the only way he could do it was by sacrificing his own life.

Hadfield told the court he had thought long and hard about what God had told him. Suicide was the obvious answer to the dilemma but he had ruled that out because he thought it was wicked to take your own life and, if you did, you went to hell. So then he hit upon the idea of killing the King. That way, he reckoned, he would be swiftly executed. It would all be over very quickly, he would have done what God had told him to do and he would have saved the world. He was only carrying out what he saw as his 'divine mission'.

All of this left the judge with a problem. Hadfield was clearly guilty, he said, but he couldn't sentence him to be hanged because he was obviously insane. The humane thing to do would be to lock him away. The problem was, where? Prison wasn't the ideal answer, but where else could he go? Normally lunatics were sent to a place called Bethlem Hospital, which later came to be known as Bedlam, but the judge said he couldn't send him there because there wasn't enough security, and Hadfield had told the police officers who arrested him that, wherever he was sent, he would try to escape and finish off the job God had given him to do. In other words, he was still determined to kill the King.

The judge said he had no alternative but to send Hadfield to prison but also said that he was doing it without legal justification because, in the eyes of the law, the insane should be treated as innocent. Furthermore, said the judge, all the other certified lunatics in jail at the time – and there were many of them – shouldn't have been there. They should be placed in a lunatic asylum built especially to deal with them.

The case, and the judge's comments, caused uproar and,

within weeks, the government passed the Criminal Lunatics Act of 1800. Under it, anyone found guilty but insane could be held in custody 'until His Majesty's Pleasure be known'. And a Select Committee of the House of Commons recommended that 'a building should be erected for the separate confinement of all persons detained under the Criminal Lunatics Act'.

And that is how Broadmoor came into being – all because of a madman who tried to kill the King. The story, though, did not have a happy ending for King George. He spent the final years of his life confined to his palace with mental illness under medical supervision.

And James Hadfield? Well, it wasn't a happy ending for him, either. He lived another forty-one years, until 23 January 1841, when he died, still under lock and key, at the age of sixty-nine. He never did manage to save the world.

It also seems that the government of the day didn't act any more quickly than modern governments over the business of sorting out people's health. It took them until 1856, fifty-six years after Hadfield had made his ill-fated attempt at regicide, to give the official go-ahead for the building of a special asylum for the criminally insane. It was to be called Broadmoor because, presumably, it was going to be built on a broad moor in Berkshire. And it took them another seven years, to 1863, before they built it. In all those years in between they put all criminal madmen (and women) in extra buildings they had erected at Bethlem Hospital and at Fisherton House, an asylum near Salisbury in Wiltshire.

Broadmoor, thirty-five miles from London, was to be the country's first state institution for mentally abnormal offenders. Rampton, in Nottinghamshire, which some people believe to be the oldest such establishment, wasn't built until 1910. Inmates at Broadmoor used to be known as HMPs (His/Her Majesty's Pleasure) and, unofficially, as 'Pleasuremen'. There was, though, never any pleasure in being sent to either Broadmoor or Rampton and the term has now died out.

Quite why the authorities placed Broadmoor where they did is uncertain but presumably in those days few people lived in the area, even though it wasn't far from London and civilization. The hospital is set on a high ridge less than a mile from Crowthorne in the middle of the Berkshire pine forests. Its close neighbour is Wellington College, about a mile away. Broadmoor is set on top of the ridge and the college is in the valley below it. The story goes that the asylum and the college were built at about the same time and had to decide between them who should have which site. According to an official document of the time, 'The boys are more fitted to play football on a flat surface – the lunatics like to look at the landscape.' So Broadmoor went to the top of the ridge.

The view from the terrace at the back of the hospital is spectacular and standing on it you can see for miles and miles, as far as the beautiful countryside of Hampshire and Surrey, way in the distance. The architect was Sir Joshua Jebb, who also designed Pentonville prison. Prisons and institutions were his speciality, although beauty of design certainly wasn't. Broadmoor is an ugly place: tall, severe blocks with barred windows, built in dark red bricks. The boundary walls are huge, making even the gardens feel claustrophobic. If Jebb designed this place to be intimidating, he succeeded. If he felt that his creation would – even for a moment – lift the spirits of the poor souls locked inside it, then he failed, miserably.

Most of the building was done by convicts and, even after the first patients arrived in 1863, the convicts carried on working for another couple of years. Jebb designed the hospital so that it would be totally self-contained and self-sufficient; it would need to have little contact with the world outside. The hospital has its own water supply and sewage plant, kitchens, gardens, small farm, and workshops for tailoring, carpentry and metalwork. There is even a cemetery here and the coffins for those who die are made by patients in the carpentry shop. Even the burial service is carried out inside the hospital, which has its own chapel.

Ralph Partridge wrote about the cemetery: 'There are flowers on some of the graves. But the old cemetery, where 1445 of the dead lie buried under matted grass, numbered from left to right as if on parade, is one of the saddest places on earth.'

One of the many sad souls who died in Broadmoor was called Billy Giles and he sums up the hopelessness that this place has meant for hundreds of its inmates. According to the records, Giles was sent here in 1886 for setting fire to a haystack. Is that really the crime of a raving lunatic? The authorities apparently thought so, because Billy Giles never got out. He died, still a patient, in 1962. Seventy-six years inside this place for setting fire to a haystack, apparently in a fit of pique after an argument with a farmer. It cost him very dear.

Many patients have been in Broadmoor for thirty years or more, often for minor crimes. An official government document states that as many as 50 per cent of patients over the years should never have been sent here in the first place. About one hundred patients are discharged every year, but many won't leave until they are decrepit – or dead. On average, twelve people die here every year. Perhaps it is not surprising, then, against such a background, that there has been a lot of violence here, much of it directed against those in charge. These days they call the top man the general manager, but he used to be the superintendent. In the eyes of the inmates, he has always been the symbol of the authority which put them inside here.

Violence was directed in 1863 at the first superintendent, Dr John Meyer. Within a few weeks of his arrival there was a mass escape from the 'strong box', where the most dangerous patients were (and still are) kept. They were all recaptured but discontent simmered within the hospital walls. The patients were not happy in their new surroundings, or with the way they were treated – and they blamed Dr Meyer. Eventually and inevitably there came an attempt to murder him.

It happened when the doctor and his family were attending a service of Holy Communion in the hospital chapel. A patient rushed forward and struck him a severe blow on the head with a large stone wrapped in a handkerchief. Dr Meyer's life was saved by one of the nurses who saw what was happening and managed to divert the full force of the blow by throwing himself between the doctor and his attacker. But Dr Meyer was apparently never the same man after the incident and died less than seven years later in 1870. It was claimed by his family and friends that his death was accelerated by the after-effects of the blow he received.

The few local residents had been alarmed by the mass escape of patients from the 'strong box' and complaints were made to MPs and newspapers. But shortly after, two inmates, Daniel McLean and Alice Kaye, made permanent escapes from Broadmoor.

In those early years, male patients were kept in six blocks and female patients in two. In all there were about four hundred people in the hospital. It was impersonal and inhuman and all patients were known by their serial numbers. When they came here they virtually ceased to exist as individuals. They had no visitors, no names, no identity, just a number. They were truly better off dead. When they died the serial number, not their name, was engraved on the tombstone. Before the dead were buried, though, their brains were removed so that the hospital doctors could dissect and study them in a bid to learn more about insanity and what caused it.

One brain they would doubtless have enjoyed dissecting, though they never had the chance, was that of a particularly violent murderer called William Bisgrove. He made history by becoming the only murderer to escape successfully from Broadmoor, and even his flight was marked by violence. On 12 July 1873, Bisgrove attacked a nurse while he was out exercising in the grounds, clambered over the garden wall and ran off into the woods surrounding the hospital. He was never seen again. After his escape security was greatly tightened up and freedom of movement became even more restricted.

But the unhappiness of the patients and the violence against senior members of staff continued even after the demise of the ill-fated Dr Meyer, who was replaced as superintendent by Dr Orange. In 1882 Dr Orange was attacked by the Reverend H. J. Dodwell, a genuine man-of-the-cloth who had become mad and had been inside Broadmoor for four years after attempting to shoot the Master of the Rolls. He had failed in that attempt and also failed to kill Dr Orange, though the latter was forced to retire through ill health shortly after.

This attack resulted in an official investigation into why the patients were venting their anger on hospital officials. The report which followed concluded: 'In the lunatic domain the Superintendent acts the role of the king. The inmates see themselves as victims of injustice and authority. The inmates see the Superintendent as the Authority. That is why they attack him. They rarely attack each other.'

The report was correct in its conclusion that patients 'rarely attack each other', because that is true. But there are always exceptions to every rule: in 1946 one patient hit another on the head with a bottle and killed him. It is not surprising that those early patients became so upset. There was no kindness or therapy, in those days, and they were simply caged and treated like animals, probably rather worse. There was also much use of mechanical restraints, padded cells and strait-jackets. Even the official description of the strait-jackets used years ago at Broadmoor has a chilling sound to it: 'Boiler suits of stout canvas fastened behind the neck. Material stiff enough to impede brusque movements and tough enough to prevent the wearer from tearing it to ribbons.'

Nothing changed for the better until 1920 and the arrival of a superintendent called Dr Sullivan. He appears to have been the first man in the history of the hospital who cared about trying to make the patients happy and trying to make them better. He started experimenting with therapy and rehabilitation and also with drugs to calm upset patients. Even in his reign, though, Broadmoor was still a primitive place. Razors were forbidden and all of the patients were unshaven. That alone must have led to them being uncaring about their appearance. The no-shaving rule did not change until as recently as 1944, and then only in some blocks.

Patients' visits, from relatives and friends, a vital part of the rehabilitation of every inmate, weren't introduced until 1926. Until then, the moment you were locked inside the hospital you lost all contact with the outside world, except by letter. Visiting was introduced by Dr Foulerton who replaced Dr Sullivan in 1926, and relatives were allowed to see patients on one Sunday every month. Sadly it seems that many didn't receive any visitors, such was the stigma attached to mental illness in those unenlightened days. Many people were ashamed to have relations inside the hospital and to be seen entering it. Few cared to admit they had a husband, father, or other relation who was mad. They simply ignored them and stayed away.

The first real Broadmoor revolution probably started under Dr Hopwood who took over as superintendent during the Second World War and stayed until 1952. Hopwood introduced electric shock treatment – and sport. Suddenly patients who had been more or less confined to their blocks apart from a daily supervised walk were allowed to play football, basketball and bowls. Later, they were even allowed to take part in whist drives, and occasional dances to which the hospital's female inmates were also invited. A choral society was formed – concert parties took place from time to time – and even a drama group, The Broadhumoorists, who still put on plays today. Four thousand people see their shows every year, including many members of the general public, although the cast has to adopt fictitious names. They do comedies, drama, which sometimes involves stage murders, and even Shakespeare. These days the actors are sometimes coached by professional actors and members of the Royal Shakespeare Company, who give up their spare time, free of charge, to come to the hospital to give advice. When that news got out recently some people, including the local MP Andrew

McKay, claimed it was an outrage and should be stopped immediately. The present Broadmoor management, however, allowed the visits by professional actors to continue.

The introduction of electro-convulsive therapy (ECT), otherwise known as electric shock treatment, proved to be highly controversial. Shock treatment in its most primitive form is one of the oldest treatments for the insane: it dates back to the eighteenth century when lunatics were given regular whippings and floggings to jolt them out of their madness. Whether it worked, or whether it was simply good sport for the whippers and the watchers, is impossible to know, but it was a popular attraction, and 'people used to flock to a place called Bedlam to watch the spectacle'. Therein, of course, lies the origin of the expression 'to create bedlam'. Eventually, of course, this kind of treatment was seen for what it really was, primitive and barbaric, and sedative drugs have been improved and developed. But the use of electric shock as a treatment for insanity has been widespread and it is still used today in a number of prisons and mental hospitals. The treatment is supposedly quite humane, though some patients do not agree.

Certainly, ECT hasn't always been humane. Ralph Partridge witnessed a patient at the hospital receiving ECT some forty years ago. His description of it is quite chilling – and he was writing from a pro-Broadmoor viewpoint:

The patient was lying on the floor of a corridor of Block One on a mattress in his pyjamas, covered with a blanket. The ECT is portable and can be used anywhere in the institution where there is a power plug.

He was a powerful man of about thirty-five with a rugged face and one of those twisted expressions commonly met in the Back Blocks. He held out his hand to the doctor and insisted on greeting me, too, with a cordial handshake.

He showed no agitation whatsoever. The ECT was

already in place behind the man's head – a small instrument not larger than a portable wireless.

The doctor plugged the cable in and turned a knob, when a needle on a dial began to turn. 'One needn't understand the electrical part of it,' said the doctor, 'but the correct dose for this man is when the needle registers 25 on the gauge.' A plastic loop, in the shape of a telephonist's headphone, was then passed under the patient's neck, bringing two wads of lint in a tight fit against his temples on either side. The electric current is to pass from one wad of lint to the other across his forehead and the lint is wetted with a salt solution to ensure a good contact. A thin cylinder of rubber wrapped in lint was put across his mouth like a bit, for him to clench with his teeth. The doctor had explained briefly to me beforehand what was going to happen: the actual shock would last the merest fraction of a second and the man would never be conscious of it but would go straight off into a characteristic epileptic fit. Two male nurses were kneeling beside him, one with hands on his shoulders, the other on his legs.

I half expected some sound from the machine as the shock was given, but it is quite silent and the only sign of it is the abrupt change in the man. The face is contorted, the eyes roll up until they almost disappear, an arm begins to swing across the chest with a jerky, automatic motion; the knees rise and fall spasmodically. The male nurses control these bodily exertions firmly and gently, while the doctor holds the chin up with his right hand to prevent any chance of the mouth opening, when he might dislocate his lower jaw or bite his tongue. The doctor, who has given over a thousand ECTs without mishap, draws my attention to the colour of the man's face, which is turning blue, because he has stopped breathing and his oxygen is exhausted. This is normal and gives no cause for alarm. In case of need an oxygen cylinder is standing within easy reach.

The paroxysm lasts for some two minutes; and then the eyes roll down, the limbs become quiescent and the bluish tinge leaves the face as the man starts to breathe again. A slight froth appears over the roll in his mouth, as he puffs out after each breath.

'In a moment he will start trying to sit up in a confused state, as he recovers consciousness,' predicts the doctor.

And so he does. With eyes open, but unfocused, the patient in a dazed way heaves himself into a sitting position and then gently sinks back again, while the nurses adjust the blanket over him. The ECT is over and the whole process has lasted ten minutes.

'This man will probably stay awake,' says the doctor, 'but in cases of depression the patients generally go off to sleep.' Schizophrenics and epileptics are not regarded as the most likely to benefit from shock treatment. It is for the depressed phase of manic-depressive insanity that ECT is specially recommended: the thread of morbid imagination is broken by shock and it is hoped the patient may return to consciousness afterwards, almost literally a 'new' man. Before ECT little could be done for such depressed cases, who tended to sink lower and lower in the grip of their despondency until completely demented . . .

There is no accounting for the consequences of ECT. Doctors go on using it with confidence, not because they understand its electrical influence on the human brain, but because in a flash and without any further argument it can persuade a man to stop shredding his jacket or to eat up his porridge.

In other cases, ECT hasn't gone so well: patients' bodies have jumped in the air with the shock, and limbs have been broken. There was also a sad case, in 1991, of a mental hospital patient

at a hospital in ....
told an inquest, ...
treatment by ECT. ......

As already me....... ....
shock treatment to Bro........ ....
hospital in 1952. Since ....
superintendents or general ....
ECT and the increasing use ....
been the subject of attacks. O...... ....
a patient called Mick Peterson, ...he
roof of Somerset House that the .... .acuated
from the block for some weeks whil..... .... .moved in to
repair it.

There have been, and continue to ..., a number of attacks
on nurses. A patient named John Silvers spent the best part of
fourteen years in the punishment block because he kept punching
nurses on the chin and another, Mike Smithers, attempted to
bite off a nurse's ear. A nurse complained recently about the
number of times he has been attacked: 'The bastards always go
for my knees, and if it happens much more they're going to
cripple me.'

Ralph Partridge described the buildings at Broadmoor well
but if he were able to come back to the hospital now he would
be amazed by the new buildings but also to find that many of the
old buildings which he described are still standing and in use.
The old buildings are grim. Each stands on three storeys with a
single staircase connecting the three floors. On each floor a broad
passage covered with linoleum runs the whole length of the
block. The patients' rooms are along these corridors, small rooms
with bars at the windows. There is just enough room for a bed, a
small table and a chair. Each floor has its own communal
washroom, and several sets of locked gates so that patients can
be isolated if trouble breaks out. The entrance floor to each of
the seven blocks is double-locked, even during the daytime, with
two separate keys, quite a contrast to the new blocks.

th no view of the gardens, are
y are where the so-called 'bad cases'
nd floor are the old patients in the last
ath. You will see them, often wrapped in
sitting and staring through the windows. For them
no hope, and death, when it comes, will be a blessing.

On the first and second floors are the dangerous cases. Few, if any, 'outsiders' are ever allowed to see inside these wards, which smell strongly of human excreta. Some of the patients refuse to eat and have to be tube-fed. Others are in such a state of hopelessness that they become limp, rather like rag dolls. The great dancer Nijinsky is said to have spent years like that locked away in an asylum. Those who suffer from epilepsy are kept well away from the windows in case they break the glass and try to use it to slash themselves. The chamber pots are made of rubber for the same reason. All of these blocks have their own private airing courts for exercise.

The Solitary Block, for patients in solitary confinement, also has its own airing court, a semi-circular open space, surrounded by a high wall. It is completely bare except for a wooden bench with its legs firmly set in concrete, and there is graffiti on the walls. You get some sad cases in the Special Blocks, people who think they are royalty and suchlike. One man believed the rest of the world was three days behind him. He wouldn't read newspapers because he thought they were three days out of date. There's also what they call the 'Broadmoor noise': the endless constant chanting of patients who are unhappy, who believe they have grievances and grudges which no one will listen to.

Five of the seven blocks – or houses as they are called – date back to the original hospital. They have been adapted and improved since those archaic times, but if any patients of 1863 were able to come back now, they would still be able to recognize the place they knew. A terrible indictment on society and the many governments who've been in power in the past 130 years.

Change is beginning slowly to happen. Now there are two

new ward blocks: Oxford House, which comprises Abingdon, Banbury, Woodstock and Henley Wards in a total of ninety rooms, and Bedford House, which has twenty-five rooms, a medical centre and an infirmary. That's a maximum of 125 patients and when you think that in January 1991 there were 497 patients here (387 male, 110 female), that still leaves an awful lot of them housed in the old buildings.

The new development at Broadmoor also includes a main kitchen and domestic services building, offices for staff and a refurbished shop which is run by the hospital's League of Friends. There is also a gymnasium, which Sir Jimmy Savile opened in 1991 after helping to raise the money to pay for it.

Jimmy Savile is a remarkable man who is a voluntary helper at Broadmoor. He doesn't pay lip service to the job either. He's here a lot listening to patients' problems and joining them in various activities. He's very well thought of by the patients and staff because of his cheerful manner and because he does a lot of fund-raising for the hospital. Occasionally he says some outrageous things – he once told the press, 'All of the people here aren't bad, but they are all mad!' – but we forgive him for the occasional indiscretion.

More new buildings are planned at Broadmoor although, for the time being, the money has run out. But, when money is available, one of the old blocks, Kent House, will be refurbished so that the seventy-five patients in there can have their own toilet facilities.

Therapy and rehabilitation are improving, too, and we now have a Director of Rehabilitation. The treatment now available includes chemotherapy, psychotherapy and, they say, more sophisticated medication. You still hear accusations, though, that the nursing staff are a bit too free and easy with drugs to keep some of the patients under control.

In March 1991 the Princess of Wales came to visit Broadmoor at her own request. This caused a lot of excitement within the hospital. She did a great service in coming because it drew the right kind of media attention to the hospital for a change. It is important that the public are made aware of what happens here, important they know that the inmates are human beings who need help.

Broadmoor publishes its own magazine every month, which is written and edited by the patients themselves. The *Broadmoor Chronicle* has been produced since 1944 and while it is censored by the management – articles are not permitted to be over-critical of the hospital and the treatment carried out – the writers are still given plenty of freedom. It contains a lot of humour, including jokes and cartoons, and poetry, because many patients find that writing poetry is helpful therapy.

Broadmoor is a self-contained place and the patients make of their lives the best they can. Ralph Partridge wrote of Broadmoor, 'My opinion is that it is a place for any nation to be proud of.' That statement is open to conjecture, and it is likely that fifty years from now, Broadmoor will probably not exist in its present form. The way forward has to be in much smaller, more specialized hospitals. But Partridge also wrote, 'Possibly we are all closer to Broadmoor than we like to think. In the opinion of a man who has intimate knowledge of more than two thousand murderers, sane and insane: "There is none of us who is not capable of murder under certain circumstances."' It is also true that the dividing line between sanity and insanity is narrow. Very narrow indeed. A high percentage of the people who read this book will, one day, suffer from some form of mental illness.

What happens now to the story of Broadmoor? There must be enormous change in the British penal system in prisons and special hospitals before there is anarchy and destruction. The Conservative government realized this in 1991 – finally – and in February of that year Lord Justice Wolf set the prison reform agenda for the rest of this century, and the beginning of next, when he published proposals to restore decency and justice into jails where conditions had become intolerable.

His recommendations also reflected conditions at many of

Britain's specialist penal establishments, such as Broadmoor. Indeed, just a few months later, the government revealed that it planned to spend 'millions' on Broadmoor. It also said it now accepted that as many as 50 per cent of patients inside the hospital should not have been there at all, and should never have been committed to such a harsh regime. Finally, plans are afoot eventually to move many of these patients to as yet unbuilt special secure hospitals. How long all of this will take is anybody's guess but, at least, and at long last, there is hope.

At the centre of Lord Wolf's 600-page report on the riot at Strangeways jail in Manchester, is a plan to convert most of the prison system into a network of community prisons, closer to the big towns and cities. Each jail would hold no more than four hundred inmates and the larger establishments would be split up into two or more prisons, each operating within the same perimeter fence. This is common sense – so why did it take the riot at Strangeways to make it obvious to those who run the country? And why did it take a costly investigation by Lord Justice Wolf officially to state the obvious?

Prisoners will welcome Lord Wolf's recommendation that 'A new prison rule should establish that no establishment should exceed its certified capacity by more than 3 per cent for more than seven days in any three months.' One of the main causes of trouble in Britain's jails in recent years has been overcrowding. It makes life hell for both the prisoners and the men who have to supervise them. This is not helped by the fact that Britain has fewer prison officers than any other major European country. Fewer officers – but far more prisoners. It's all been dangerously out of balance.

Other aspects of the Wolf Report are to be welcomed, such as the suggestion that prisoners should receive a formal contract stating what the prison was expected to provide and what was expected from the prisoner in return. And, if the prisoner felt his expectations of the prison were not fulfilled, he could invoke grievance procedures and, as a last resort, seek judicial review.

Lord Wolf also wisely recommended that offenders be put in jails close to home, so that their relations can visit them more easily and some sort of family life can be maintained.

Home Secretary Kenneth Baker has promised to abolish 'slopping out' in all prisons and special hospitals by the end of 1994. This degrading practice should have been ended many years ago. Mr Baker also promised measures to improve inmates' family ties, including extra visits and home leaves, the abolition of routine censorship of mail (at Broadmoor *every* letter sent or received by a patient is opened and read by the hospital), and the provision of cardphones for use at prisoners' own expense.

A lot of promises but perhaps the words of Lord Justice Wolf and Judge Stephen Tumim, the Chief Inspector of Prisons and joint author of the report, that 'it should be regarded as a complete package', and that ministers should not choose 'only some ingredients', will be heeded.

Kenneth Baker said, 'Prison is not supposed to be a holiday camp, but nor should it degrade and humiliate. Jails should be austere but decent, providing a busy but positive regime.'

Bibliography

I have read a lot of books about crime, Broadmoor, etc., and I have borrowed a small amount of information from some of them, plus some quotations. I acknowledge my debt to the following books:

Reg Kray, *Born Fighter*, Century Books, 1991

Tony Lambrianou, *Inside the Firm*, Smith Gryphon, 1991

Brian McConnell, Tum Tullett and Edward Vale, *The Evil Firm*, Mayflower, 1969

Ralph Partridge, *Broadmoor – A History of Criminal Lunacy and Its Problems*, Chatto & Windus

Leonard Read with James Morton, *Nipper*, Macdonald, 1992

Scene Out, Archway Publishing, (magazine)

Reg and Ron Kray
with Fred Dinenage
Our Story £5.99

The Kray twins were Britain's most notorious gangsters. For a decade they were the gang lords of the London underworld.

Their reign of terror ended on March 8 1969 when Ronnie and Reg were sentenced to life with the recommendation that they serve at least thirty years.

Today Ronnie languishes in Broadmoor – his raging insanity only controlled by massive doses of drugs. Reg has served two decades in some of Britain's toughest jails.

But the men whose name was a byword for fear have never revealed the truth about their violent life and times – until now. In *Our Story*, they set the record straight. In their own words they tell the full story of their brutal careers in crime and their years behind bars.

Compiled from a series of interviews behind prison walls, *Our Story* is the book that finally explodes the myths that have surrounded the Kray twins.

'Reminds the reader that a penal system that does not attempt to rehabilitate the sick in mind is always going to fail the society it aims to protect. The Krays, it would be fair to say, have been left to rot'
THE OBSERVER

'A fascinating social document . . . Reg is fiercely, bitterly sane and his stocial endurance of 20 years' incarceration with another ten to go has a gloomy dignity which commands respect and makes his and his brother's account of their lives worth reading'
THE SPECTATOR

'An astonishing book . . . you will be astounded by the frankness of the Krays' own chilling story of crime'
THE SUN